W9-CZN-123

Alicia Afterimage

A story of friendship, healing, and remembrance

LULU DELACRE

LEE & LOW BOOKS Inc.

New York

Royalties from the sale of this book will be split between the Alicia Betancourt Prize for Excellence in the Arts, a scholarship awarded yearly to a female Blake High School senior with a strong interest in the visual arts and/or dance, and a charitable fund that awards grants to people and causes that Alicia's parents believe their daughter would support.

Pronunciation and definition of the word *afterimage* on page iii from *Merriam-Webster's Collegiate Dictionary*, eleventh ed. Springfield, MA: Merriam-Webster, Incorporated, 2004. Song lyrics in chapter 10 (pages 65–70) from "A Perfect Mourn" by Ben Holgash. Used with permission. Poem on page 75 from *Margarita* by Rubén Darío, is in the public domain. Song lyrics on page 86 from "Feliz, feliz en tu día" by Emilio Aragón Bermúdez. Used with permission.

Messages on pages 14–15 and 114–115 from tributes written on a scroll at Blake High School. Photographs on pages 21 and 108 by Lulu Delacre. Used with permission. Photograph on pages 125 and 137 by Lauren Perry. Used with permission. All other photographs, and all drawings, crafts, and collages, by Alicia María Betancourt. Used with permission of Lulu Delacre.

LEE & LOW BOOKS Inc., 95 Madison Avenue, New York, NY 10016
leeandlow.com
Manufactured in the United States of America
by Worzalla Publishing Company, September 2017
Book production by The Kids at Our House
The text is set in Meridien

(hc) 10 9 8 7 6 5 4 3 2 1
(pb) 10 9 8 7 6 5 4 3 2 1
First Edition

Library of Congress Cataloging-in-Publication Data
Delacre, Lulu.
Alicia afterimage / by Lulu Delacre. — 1st ed.
p. cm.
Summary: Explores the life of Alicia, a popular sixteen-year-old, in the aftermath of a fatal car crash, as her friends, family members, and others recall key episodes that show her impact on their lives. Includes author's note about the real Alicia and how she inspired the book, as well as resources on teen grief.
ISBN 978-1-60060-242-9 (hardcover) ISBN 978-1-62014-578-4 (paperback)
[1. Death—Fiction. 2. Grief—Fiction. 3. Friendship—Fiction. 4. Family life—Maryland—Fiction. 5. Traffic accidents—Fiction. 6. Puerto Ricans—Fiction. 7. Maryland—Fiction.] I. Title.
PZ7.D3696Ali 2008
[Fic]—dc22   2007042158

af·ter·im·age (ˈaf-tər-ˌi-mij) *noun*: a usually visual sensation occurring after stimulation by its external cause has ceased

To all grieving teens

CHAPTER 1

Mamá

Mamá sprang up in bed, eyes wide-open. A helicopter droned in the distance on the balmy September night. She put on her glasses.

"What time is it?" she asked her husband.

"I thought you were asleep." Papá set down his book and turned to glance at the alarm clock. "It's eleven thirty."

"I have to call Alicia," Mamá said, picking up her cell phone from the nightstand. She scrolled down to her younger daughter's name and sent the call through. The phone rang one, two, three, four times before the voice mail message came on. That was odd. When Alicia's phone was on, she always answered it. She loved being in touch.

Mamá got up and looked out the window. Across the street,

a neighbor's television flickered in a second-floor bedroom.

"Don't worry," Papá said. "They may be in an area with poor reception."

Mamá scanned beyond the rooftops, breathing deeply to stay calm. She sensed the reason was otherwise. She was sure of it. . . .

"Mami, can I go—please? Please?" Alicia stood eagerly by the stove. The aroma of shrimp in garlic sauce drifted through the kitchen.

Earlier that Friday evening a boy from school called Alicia to invite her out. They didn't know what they were going to do. Maybe they would go to the movies at the mall in Olney, Alicia said.

"¿Mami?"

Mami, Mamá thought. The term of endearment touched her.

"Why don't you ask him to come visit you here, after dinner?" Mamá suggested. She tasted the garlic sauce and adjusted the seasonings. She had wanted to prepare something Alicia relished. Mamá knew that Alicia always looked forward to dinner as a highlight in her day.

"You could play pool in the basement," Mamá added.

"No, Mamá," Alicia said. "That's boring."

"Déjala ir," Papá said, intervening. "Let her go."

Now that Alicia was a junior in high school Mamá wanted to give her more freedom, but it was hard to balance freedom and protection. Mamá wanted Alicia to make her own choices, but she did not want her daughter to get hurt in any way.

Mamá checked the rice and stirred the shrimp once more. This boy was a senior, the Digital Arts teacher's assistant. He had relatives in the neighborhood, whom he visited on weekends. Just the night before, Mamá had been at the school's football game to watch Alicia dance at halftime. After the performance Alicia had taken Mamá by the hand and brought her to the fence where the boy was standing with a friend. Alicia introduced him to Mamá; and when they walked away, Alicia confided, "I think he likes me."

Looking at Alicia now, Mamá found herself enveloped by her daughter's warm smile. It was a hard-to-resist smile, the kind that makes you feel happy all over for no reason.

"Well, maybe you could go bowling or to the ice cream parlor," Mamá said, relenting. "But I don't want you out too late, and be sure to tell that boy to come to the door to pick you up. We want to talk to him."

"Yea!" Alicia flung her arms in the air. Having won permission, she proceeded to haggle over her curfew during dinner. They all agreed on eleven thirty.

By one thirty in the morning, Mamá and Papá had spent almost two hours calling their daughter's friends, nearby hospitals, and the police. Papá then drove to the boy's house. Mamá stayed home in case someone called. She jumped when the phone rang about an hour later. It was Papá. He said that everyone had been asleep when he got to the boy's house, and the boy was not yet home. While Mamá and Papá talked, the police contacted the boy's parents: The car had been totaled, and the boy had been flown from the crash site. Papá told Mamá he had to go. The police officers were coming over to see him.

Thinking about the officers getting out of their patrol car and approaching Papá compelled Mamá to call him. He was already on his way home. Mamá wanted to hear the words. When Papá broke down in tears and told her, it didn't surprise her. Mamá had known it in her heart. She didn't even cry. "Alicia is with God" was all she said.

Right then Mamá stopped worrying about her cherished daughter. For sixteen years Mamá had worried day and night about a million things. She worried about her daughter's health, diet, safety, studies, values, friends, and after-school activities. Her latest worry had been about the physics teacher. Was he good enough to give Alicia a strong science foundation? Alicia had voiced an interest in studying interior architecture. She needs physics for that, Mamá had thought.

As those worries lifted and vanished, a vacuum took their place. In it questions arose. What happens now? Does life continue? Do I keep on living? And if I do, how?

When Papá arrived home, Mamá could hardly absorb his words. He said that the officers had followed him when he left the boy's house. They had been intent on making sure he didn't drive to the crash site. Papá had wanted to go there, but a police investigator said it would be too painful and haunting. So Papá suggested that the investigator take the boy's school yearbook and use Alicia's picture in it to make the identification.

At four thirty the investigator called Mamá and Papá to confirm their worst fears. The dead passenger was indeed their daughter Alicia. The yearbook picture, and the Baltimore crab charm of her name that dangled from the keys in the passenger's purse, had been enough to make a positive ID. He said that the boy was in the Shock Trauma Center in Baltimore. Going more than twenty miles above the speed limit in a standard-shift car he had only driven for the last few weeks, the boy had lost control. The car slid into the embankment. The boy overcorrected and sent the car into a spin. On the poorly lit country road, about a five-minute drive from Alicia's home, the car hit a telephone pole on the passenger's side.

Months later, when Mamá read the final police report, she found out that according to the autopsy, her slender, four-feet-eleven-inch daughter had died instantly, with her seat belt on. There had been no drugs, no alcohol. Speeding and inexperience were listed as the causes.

Lying in bed for the next couple of hours in their dark and suddenly empty home, Mamá and Papá hugged in silence. So many questions crowded Mamá's mind. How would they tell

Verónica that her little sister had died? How could they deliver such news in a long-distance telephone call? Life had handed Mamá and Papá a situation they had no idea how to approach. Paralyzed, they waited for dawn. Maybe daylight would bring the answers.

CHAPTER 2

Papá awoke from a restless sleep around three in the morning. It was Tuesday, four days after the accident; and in six hours the limousine from the funeral parlor would arrive. He had set aside the suit and tie he would wear. He still needed to get his speech ready. . . .

Since Saturday the house had felt like an airport, bursting with people, well-meaning people, coming and going. They had brought salads and casseroles. There had been awkward words, tears, silences, hugs. Dozens of tissue boxes decorated with Disney characters popped up and spread throughout the living room, family room, and kitchen.

Papá had been forced to make many decisions in a very short time. On Saturday morning he arranged for Verónica to fly home from Italy, where she had just started the fall semester of her junior year of college. He dreaded that something might happen to his older daughter on her way home. In the afternoon a friend had taken him and Mamá to the funeral home. When the double doors opened to reveal more than fifteen gleaming caskets showcased like jewels, Papá shivered. There had been packages and options from which to choose. There had been prices so high, he wondered how anybody could afford them. Did he really have to choose a box for *his* Alicia? This was one task he hadn't cared to master. In the end he let his wife do the choosing.

"I want the simplest box," Mamá said. "And why do we need a metal lining in the hole? Why can't the pine box go directly into the earth?"

"It's a requirement of the cemetery," the funeral home employee answered. "So the ground doesn't shift."

"What do you mean?" Mamá looked puzzled.

"If there is no metal lining the ground caves in quickly." The employee straightened his tie. "It's harder to mow."

Harder to mow?

———

Papá went to the basement, turned on the computer, and began to write. The words seeped out of his heart and onto the screen slowly but decisively. How could he say all that Alicia meant to him? The three of them—Papá, Mamá, and Verónica—

had agreed the night before that they would each speak at the funeral mass. They had been allotted a total of about twenty minutes, but it would take however long it would take.

Papá heard his wife's light steps on the stairs. "Are you writing your eulogy?" Mamá asked, peeking in. Papá nodded.

"I can't sleep. I think I'll work on mine too," Mamá said.

Papá then saw Verónica come into the room. Verónica said she had been awake in bed and, upon hearing noises, she followed them downstairs.

"I have to go last," Papá warned. "When we speak at church, I have to go last. Either one of you can go first." He stared at the screen and kept tapping the keys. *Alicia touched so many of us in so many different ways that we all have our special Alicia memory, one that she gave only to each and every one of us.* Tears blurred his vision. Then, remembering, a chuckle filled his throat. . . .

"Okay," said Alicia, gently pushing aside the baby spinach leaves her mother insisted on serving her. "Now I'll show you the latest Poms routine." Only last year Papá had learned that these high school dancing teams were named after the pom-poms their members were required to use in their performances.

Alicia jumped up from her seat, picked up her plate, and took it to the sink. Then she stood in the middle of the kitchen and announced the songs to which the squad would be dancing.

"*Ay,* Mamá," Alicia said when Mamá complained about not recognizing any of the songs. Papá always knew them. He listened to the same radio station as Alicia. He liked some of his daughter's favorite bands, and had even gone to a concert with her.

The routine consisted of many sharp and quick movements. Alicia marched, twirled, and slid into splits, all the while explaining the placement and dance moves of her twenty-three teammates. She leaped into the air with such energy and joy. Papá found it easy to get tired watching Alicia rehearse, and hard to visualize the effect of the whole group dancing in unison.

"So, what do you think?" Alicia asked brightly, fixing up her ponytail.

"It looks complicated," said Papá.

"True." Mamá served herself the last of the salad. "But I like it very much, and you do it well."

"*Yo sé,*" Alicia said. "I know." She cocked her head in a self-satisfied way, quickly agreeing with her parents. "Okay. I have to finish my homework." Alicia glanced at Papá with a sly smile, turned around, and skipped up the stairs.

Papá laughed. Alicia had done it again. She had distracted her mother long enough to avoid eating her spinach; she was good.

When Papá, Mamá, and Verónica arrived at the church the funeral director approached the limousine. The rear window rolled down. In a soft, calming voice he told them not to come out yet. Too many people might hover around them and hinder the schedule. He would tell them when the service was about to start. Papá watched the unassuming man walk back to the church entrance. He was so gentle with them. He's fulfilled his calling, Papá thought.

They waited in the car, staring out the windows. Mamá clutched the folder with their words of remembrance. Verónica sniffled, and Papá squeezed her hand.

The church was filled beyond capacity. People were standing in the back and against the side walls, and spilling from the choir's alcove. Alicia's high school had sent two buses packed with students. Others had come with teachers or parents, as adults feared letting the teenagers drive. Both sides of the family were present. Friends from Papá's and Mamá's childhoods in Puerto Rico had come. Friends from work, friends from the neighborhood, and friends who lived far away were there. All had assembled in the church where Alicia had been baptized and confirmed, the church Alicia had attended on Sundays. Not even at the Easter service had Papá seen so many people.

The perfume of incense rose as hundreds of voices sang "On Eagle's Wings" during the entrance procession. Papá, Mamá, and Verónica followed the pallbearers and took their places in the front pew. Papá felt there and not there. He struggled to be present. The casket, draped in a white brocade cloth topped with an embroidered gold cross, stood in front of the altar by a tall, thick, burning candle. To the right of the altar the wind ensemble from Alicia's high school band had set up their instruments. Had any of them known Alicia? Papá wondered.

All three readings were short and powerful. The stocky priest, dressed in white and gold, delivered a touching sermon. When he finished he smoothed his white beard, picked up his guitar, and sang a folk song for Alicia. Papá raised an eyebrow, smiled, and nodded in approval. After Communion it was time for the words of remembrance. As Mamá, Verónica, and Papá stood, a gasp rippled through the crowd. Mamá led the group. Papá came last. He walked by the casket and touched it. A light touch, a caress almost, as if he were brushing Alicia's long, thick brown hair one last time. The three of them huddled close to one another behind the lectern.

Mamá spoke first. Her words were the words only a mother could speak, grateful to God for such a joyful child. Verónica talked about lessons to be learned from Alicia's bright personality, about wanting to be her younger sister's voice. Then, just as he had wanted, Papá went last. He took his speech, the one he had printed out double spaced and in large-sized type, and read it slowly, with effort. His voice shook twice, but he managed not to cry. Once he was finished, Papá lifted his gaze and asked all those present to stand and hug the people next to them, just like his Alicia had hugged everyone she loved. Papá saw young and old turn to one another and embrace to remember his daughter. And finally, as the wind ensemble played "Amazing Grace," tears spilled freely from his eyes.

It was a beautiful service, Mamá said to Papá as he, Mamá, and Verónica stood at the narthex of the church afterward. Papá agreed. *It was.*

A long line formed as people waited their turns to shake hands, hug them, or hand them some token of their empathy on their way out. Papá saw many teenagers stream by. There were hundreds, in fact. Could they all have known Alicia? In what ways had she touched their lives?

Alicia,

I begin with blue. Today is the day I've dreaded most. For the last two days I've had you in my head. This color is one of the two that paints/covers my insides. I am grey. Dead. Blue. Depressed. I spend every waking hour reminiscing about your unobtainable smile. Your glittering personality. And each night... I dream of all you were to me. I've written page upon page about you, Cried for an hour; a half. Babe! I miss you. I miss your dead face. I miss your smile. I miss your uncanny knack to poke at me. I miss all you are to everyone. My body has not functioned correctly. And while I know you wouldn't want me to be like this... I cannot help but feel the deepest of regret/remorse. I cannot fight through the veils of sorrow. To see your empty seat was to throw myself in front of a train. I love you! I love all you are to everyone. I can't write enough. I have poems! Songs & pure pain. I have nothing left. If only it were me. If only I can

brought to the subject of your art. So very life. In such a short time you created such amazing things. Your life was too beautiful to be gone. I will always remember Drew. G.T. Dime's Rubberbands. You; Jessie V. & me; Dan. Everyday was another chance to see you smile. Everyday I will look for your soul. Embrace the energy you let release into me. The impact you have on me is everlasting. You are truly one of those bright brightest stars in the sky went out. I wrote the greatest piece I've ever written; I am in your honor. Even after death, you are inspiration as raw as the love. You are indescribable. You are... Wow. These 7 long years.

have replayed on my head. I will always remember you afternoons. Our planting daisies on your honor. Gonna get something that last forever. A memories your honor. Remember just how beautiful you were? How you'll live forever. In our lives our heads. I lo... I miss you.

You Wi...

P.S. You always will be. Here's to 16 years of everlasting. I can't say it enough. I love & miss you.

Wow,

How do I begin to express my feelings on this simple sheet of paper. Your sweet innocent life was stolen & all I can feel is mad, annoyed & hurt. Mad that they took your life, annoyed that this is even happening & hurt that GOD would know how we all would feel & still call his angel home. Then on the other hand I'm am so happy that you will never suffer or shed a tear again! even if I never see you smile again you are truly happy & in eternal peace.

— Another signature who misses your smile

Oh babe girl, little one...
6 years flashed, all the good times, your smile the most...
twiz, French, every morning, FT, the FA... what were you thinking...
the art... oh little one I love you
Alicia, took a while but I got it

What can be said now that has not been said before?
What can be said now that will carry the weight of our meaning, our feeling?
What can be said now, but that you were joyful and joy-giving, that you were loved and more worthy of it than any...
that you will be severely missed?

Let that much, then, be said.
You will be sorely missed.
Greg

Alicia, a few years ago I had the girls over on Saturday night. We made t-shirts for class color day in your name. Jess B. was telling me about this movie about a bird. Coincidently who is reincarnated as a bird. Jess found a bird in her house and ended up keeping it. She's naming it Alicia. On Friday during practice me so glad you put the into a good mood. I was having such a crappy day + you lightened me up my to quiere. Hanno Delgates un otto in mi... hydeon! It's gonna ... practice, I ... up - yo ...

ALICIA —
I hope you were aware of how many people truly + deeply care for you. Life will continue for everyone, but for people who never met you, there will be some emptiness because you filled all our lives with love. ♡ m

Alicia,
I will nev...
you or you...

CHAPTER 3

Erin sat in front of the instant-messaging screen on her computer. It was the middle of the morning in the middle of August and too hot to be outside. A new screen popped up. It was Alicia. Alicia? She wanted Erin's phone number. She needed to talk.

Who is this girl? Erin thought. Oh yes, she was in her French class last year in ninth grade. Stephanie had spoken about her, but Erin had not talked to Alicia. Erin was not one to start a conversation with someone she didn't know.

Erin gave Alicia her phone number and turned off the computer. Seconds later the phone rang.

"Hi. This is Alicia."

"Hi."

"Are you trying out for Poms this year?" Alicia asked.

"Yeah." Erin pushed back on the chair and steadied her feet against the table. "We already had a first practice."

"WHAT?" Alicia gasped. "You already had a practice?"

"Yeah."

"What's the routine like?"

"It's like . . ." Erin stood up and walked around the room. "It's like . . . real complicated. We've spent two days learning it. Later today we'll go over the last sequence. The new coach is kind of strict."

"I didn't even know they had found a coach!" Alicia blurted out.

Erin fiddled with the silver heart hanging from her necklace. One side read: "I love you." The other side said the same thing in Greek: "S'agapo." Erin's mother had given her the pendant to remind her of their heritage.

"Yeah. They did." Erin sighed. Just last week she'd been told that a coach had finally been found. "Tryouts are tomorrow."

"Oh my gosh . . . ," said Alicia, her voice trailing off in disbelief. "Hold on. I have another call." Alicia giggled as she switched to the other call.

With school out for the summer, only a few girls, aside from former Poms, had learned about the tryouts. It had been through word-of-mouth. No wonder Alicia didn't know. Erin could sort of relate. She hadn't been able to join a dance class last year because the class was full by the time she'd found out about it. It sucked.

"I'm back," Erin heard Alicia say. "Sorry, that was a friend from middle school. So . . . you were telling me about tryouts."

"I think, maybe, I could teach you the routine," said Erin.

"Would you?" said Alicia. "Thank you! Can I come over now?"

"Yeah," Erin said, and gave her the address. As she hung up the phone, Erin couldn't believe she had just agreed to have a complete stranger come over. Especially to teach her a Poms routine. How did that happen?

Erin stared out her bedroom window. Minutes later a pale green car drove up the tree-lined street. It pulled into her driveway. She must live close, Erin thought as Alicia jumped out of the car. She was wearing a cherry-print top and sky blue shorts that read "Puerto Rico" on the butt. Alicia looked as if she was having a great day. Erin went downstairs and opened the door.

"Hi! Thanks for doing this." Alicia smiled up at Erin. "Thank you so much."

"Yeah," Erin answered. She didn't know if this was going to work. The routine was hard. They had spent, what, more than five hours over the last couple of days on it. But Alicia looked so excited.

"Should I tell my mom to pick me up in an hour?" Alicia asked.

Erin arched her eyebrows. "Sure," she said, thinking that an hour would be barely enough time to get started on the routine.

Alicia called out to her mother, then followed Erin inside to the basement.

Erin had been in Poms since the beginning of high school last year. She was serious about Poms, and she had recorded the exact songs they were going to dance to for the tryouts routine. Erin practiced a lot. Poms and synchronized swimming were the two activities she loved most.

First Erin showed Alicia some of the movements individually. She glanced at Alicia, to see if she was getting them. Then Erin showed Alicia a set of movements while counting: four marches and a leap with dance hands. Alicia repeated them within the count. Erin nodded, paused, and started again. Alicia was quick to copy her.

Erin turned on the CD player and put the moves to the music: one, two, three, four; one, two, three, four. Alicia joined in. Erin in front, Alicia behind. Alicia moved swiftly, her arms and legs not missing a beat. Erin in front, Alicia behind. For the next sequence Alicia jumped forward beside Erin: five, six, seven, eight. Erin smiled. Alicia was in step. It felt good to dance next to her. It was as if she had been part of the Poms team all along. Erin's smile grew wider. The squad needed a good dancer like Alicia.

When they stopped Erin looked at her watch. They had gone over the whole routine in forty-five minutes. Wow!

"Let's get something to drink," said Erin. On the way upstairs Alicia told Erin about the Poms members she knew from her Jazz Dance class in ninth grade. It was as if Alicia wanted to find out what she and Erin had in common.

"Are you all done?" asked Erin's mother.

"Hi, Mrs. Dunne." Alicia skipped into the kitchen. "No, no. We need to practice more. I really want to make the squad."

"Have you danced before?" Mrs. Dunne asked, while Erin gulped some ice-cold water.

"Jazz in ninth grade and ballet for almost eleven years, but I got tired of ballet," Alicia said matter-of-factly. "The part I liked best in ballet was performing, but we only had two shows a year."

"We perform a lot in Poms." Erin drank some more water. "I think you'll be good at it."

Alicia glanced at the oven clock, then turned around and started back downstairs. "Come on, Erin!" she called behind her. "Let's go over the last part again."

The way Alicia said her name felt special to Erin, as if they had known each other for a long time.

That afternoon, Erin saw that Alicia was the last girl to sign up for tryouts practice—girl number forty-five. The coach frowned at the last-minute addition. But after the audition the next day, the judges chose Alicia as one of the twenty-four squad members. Later, when Alicia told Erin, she said she had jumped up and down clapping and yelling after the coach phoned to tell her that she made the squad.

As soon as Alicia saw Erin the following morning she ran over and hugged her. It was one of those hugs where Alicia wrapped herself around the other person. A monkey hug. Erin felt all tingly. She didn't think it was possible, that a stranger one day could be a best friend two days later. But it had happened.

———

Sitting on her bed against the wall and bracing her long legs, Erin looked at the picture frame atop her dresser. Alicia had made the frame for Erin's birthday. It was painted in bright, bold colors. A collage of magazine cutouts surrounded by small, round mirrors on one side faced tiny origami paper flowers on the other. Inside the frame was a picture of both girls smiling on the evening of the homecoming football game in tenth grade. From a silvery chain draped over the frame Alicia had hung Erin's name, handcrafted out of metal and written in beautiful cursive letters. Looking at the picture, Erin felt a rush of feelings. These were new, different feelings that she was still struggling to define. A picture that was the memory of a good day now made Erin feel happy and sad at the same time. Happy to have met Alicia. Sad that she was gone.

Erin looked down at the mementos she had spread out on the blue carpet: newspaper clippings about the crash; school photos; the corsage she wore for the funeral service, dried and preserved in a plastic bag; the condolence card she got from Stephanie; the prayer card from the viewing; and the hot-pink T-shirt she had decorated in Alicia's memory with the rest of her Poms teammates. Erin placed each item back in the shoe box and slid the box underneath her bed. Then she reached for the silver heart pendant around her neck. That too reminded Erin of Alicia. On Alicia's sixteenth birthday, Erin had surprised her friend with a tiny box. Inside was a heart pendant and chain just like the one Erin's mother had given her.

I love you. *S'agapo*.

CHAPTER 4

Corrina

The cold wind was leaking into Corrina's room. Her sister had left the window cracked open, and Corrina got up to close it. This is not a good night to go out trick-or-treating, Corrina thought.

The phone rang downstairs. "It's for you, Corrina. It's Alicia," Corrina's mother called.

Corrina ran to the phone, eager to talk to Alicia. They always ended up laughing hysterically. Now that many of their friends from middle school had gone on to different schools, being with Alicia at Blake High School was a comfort. They were sort of each other's support system.

Putting the receiver to her ear, Corrina could hear Alicia

humming, slightly out of tune, to the music playing in the background. Alicia had music on all the time.

"Hi," said Corrina.

"Hi. It's me," said Alicia. "So, what are we doing tonight?"

"I'm staying put. I mean, it's, like, *cold* outside."

"But we have to do something," Alicia insisted. "This might be our last Halloween to trick-or-treat now that we're in high school. If you come over we can go around my neighborhood. I know the neighbors who give the best candy, and there are always a lot of little kids out, and we might even see some friends from school, and . . . oh wait . . . listen to this song." The music blasted through the phone.

Seconds later Alicia's voice came back. "Do you like it? I love it! So, you're coming over, right?"

"I don't know," Corrina mumbled. It was hard to turn down Alicia. "Well, I guess."

"Yes! You know our costumes should go together. It would be SO cute!"

By the time Corrina and Alicia agreed to dress up as an angel and a devil it was already five thirty and dark. Corrina was supposed to be at Alicia's house by six fifteen. She had no idea how she was going to make herself into an angel in half an hour.

Searching through a pile of old clothes, Corrina found her grandmother's worn-out, flimsy, white nylon robe. Corrina slipped it on. The lace-trimmed sleeves stopped inches above her wrists. Tied loosely at the front by its spaghetti-string sash, the robe revealed her light gray sweatpants underneath.

Corrina stared at her image in the mirror. "Is it angelic or homeless?" she asked herself. She shrugged, sighed, and was off.

When Alicia opened the door she started laughing. This prompted Corrina to do the same.

"What ARE you wearing?" Alicia giggled. "I can't even tell what you are!"

"What do you expect? I barely had any time to put something together."

Alicia looked perfect in her devil costume. She wore a bright red jumper, red horns, and vibrant red lipstick. She even had a long, pointy tail pinned to the back of her dress.

"Come on," Alicia said. "Let's fix this mess. You look terrible."

Corrina helped Alicia look around the house for things to add to her angel costume. Finally, from deep within the old dress-up basket, they dug out a white, feathered headband from one of Alicia's first ballet costumes. Alicia placed it on her friend's blonde hair.

"There," Alicia said. "Your halo." The girls posed, making comical faces, while Alicia's mother took pictures. Then they headed out the door.

Children of all ages were out that night. There was a football player, a pirate, a couple of witches, and a ballerina holding the hand of a cat. Behind the children, the adults walked carrying flashlights and steaming coffee or cold beer. They shouted warnings to their kids as cars passed by.

Alicia was so full of energy she practically bounced down the street. Corrina hurried beside her. At the corner house they ran into a little girl dressed as a princess walking with her mother. The girl's puffy gown was bubblegum pink, and her tiny tiara sparkled under the light of a garden lamppost.

"Mommy, what are they?" the little girl asked.

"Well . . ." The mother frowned as she pondered the question. "That's a devil, and that's a, I think it's a, well, hmmm . . ."

"Mommy." The girl tugged at her mother's jacket. "Tell me."

Corrina glanced at Alicia, and they burst out laughing. They laughed all the way down the driveway and for an entire block until their stomachs hurt.

Suddenly the wind picked up, and the evening got chillier. Corrina shivered as a boy dressed as a ghost went by. His costume was a white sheet with two holes cut out for the eyes. The sight of the boy reminded Alicia of something.

"Do you watch that show on TV? *Crossing Over*?" she asked.

"No. What's it about?" said Corrina.

"It's, like, a talk show. People come onstage, and the host connects them to the spirits of their loved ones. It's kind of cool. Do you think that's real?"

"No. It's all bogus." Corrina shook her head. "I don't believe in any of it."

"Well, I don't know." Alicia paused. "I think it could really happen. Getting in touch with the spirits, I mean."

Alicia turned, then pointed to a house. "Oh, look! That's where Carl lives. From English. Remember? Let's go knock on his door. I bet he'll give us lots of candy."

"Trick or treat!" the girls said in unison in their most adorable voices when Carl opened the door.

"Ah, an angel and a devil." Carl hesitated. "I think I'll have to give the angel more." He gave two handfuls of candy to Corrina and just a few pieces to Alicia before closing the door.

"Oh! I can't believe he gave you more candy!" Alicia complained. "What makes you deserve more than me?"

For the next few houses Alicia wouldn't let it go. The situation was infuriating.

Corrina laughed. It was all very funny. "Maybe we should go back and demand justice," Corrina teased.

"Excellent idea, Corrina!"

On the way back to Carl's house Alicia and Corrina planned what to say. "You have to give me more candy, or you can give me . . . YOU!" Alicia rehearsed in her most devilish voice.

"You are not going to go say that!" Corrina cried. "You wouldn't dare."

"Want to see?"

When Alicia was ready she marched up to Carl's house and rang the doorbell. Corrina stood two steps behind, covering her mouth to contain her laugh. They waited. They could see the reflection of the television screen through the window. Alicia rang a second time. She rang a third. No one answered the door, so Alicia was unable to prove she would have actually confronted Carl. Corrina didn't need proof. She knew her friend was not one to wimp out on a dare. Alicia would have done it. For sure.

Back at Alicia's house the girls warmed up with hot cocoa and then went up to Alicia's room. Seated on the carpet, they dumped out the contents of their bags and counted, traded, and ate some of their loot.

"There's this guy in my Art class; his name is Gaeb," Alicia said, savoring a crunchy chocolate morsel. "I think he's a junior. He's black and really, really funny. Anyways, he has this friend Chris. Chris is very good-looking."

"Chris? What does he look like?" Corrina asked.

"Tall, brown skin, green eyes. He hangs out in the C hall."

Corrina frowned. "The C hall?"

"Well, he wears an earring, but that doesn't mean anything, you know." Alicia stretched out her legs next to Corrina's. "Look at your feet! What size shoes do you wear?"

"Eight and a half. And look at yours, Little Miss Midget."

Alicia laughed. Corrina loved making her friend laugh, and she liked that she could talk about anything and everything with Alicia. She could be silly, quiet, witty, or anything she felt like being. She could be just plain Corrina.

More than two years later on another cold night, Corrina sat down to watch TV. The show Alicia used to watch was on, the one about connecting to the spirits of loved ones. Several months had gone by since her friend had died. During that time there had been many conversations with Alicia, all played out in Corrina's mind. Especially when Corrina was having a hard time making a decision, Alicia's voice would come on, asking questions, suggesting answers. Corrina wondered if the conversations were only imagined or if some part of them was real. She used to think there was no such thing as an afterlife. Now she didn't know what to believe. Come to think of it, it was kind of funny talking to someone who is dead. It really didn't matter, though. The truth was that Corrina felt a little less sad when she could listen to her friend in her mind. It was as if, even now, Alicia could still be with her in some way.

And at times Corrina felt Alicia was.

CHAPTER 5

Gaeb

The girl sat down next to him, and Gaeb did a double take. It was happening again. An Alicia flashback. Even here, in college, in Sociology 101. The first image he always saw was of Alicia hallway-walking, wearing, like, a little fifties' poodle skirt. Cute little Alicia. Like happy, joy, happy . . .

Spirit Week at Blake. On Tuesday the students were to dress up in outfits of their favorite decade. Alicia showed up at her fifth-period Studio Art class in a pink poodle skirt and white blouse. She sat across from Gaeb and smiled right at him. He was seated next to Justin, another eleventh grader, telling Yo' Momma jokes. Alicia laughed at each joke she overheard, her laugh lingering long after the last one.

Wow! She really thinks I'm funny, Gaeb thought. He liked to clown around. He was lanky and more than six feet tall. The role of class comic fit him.

"I haven't seen you before," Gaeb said, leaning back on his stool.

"Well, yeah. I just started high school this year," said Alicia.

"I'm Gaeb. That's *G-A-E-B*. Oh, oh—my goodness—there were so many Gabes around here when I came from Boston. So, *ahem*, I changed my name, like, the spelling."

"I know you." Alicia picked up a charcoal pencil to measure distances in the still life in front of her. "I've seen you dancing in the hallway."

Gaeb loved to dance. During lunch he and his friends would gather in the second-floor open space of the A hall to break dance. He thrived on having a circle of people watching as he moved. Gaeb would leap, split, and twirl parallel to the floor on one hand, then jump up, jerk his muscles as if popping them, and finally fall back into another split. Limber, smooth, seamless.

"May I borrow a pen?" the girl in Sociology asked. "I don't know what I did with mine."

"Yeah." Gaeb handed her a blue ballpoint. She was wearing her hair up in a short ponytail. Just like Alicia's had been in dance class . . .

They were in Intermediate Jazz, second semester, he and Alicia. Together in art and dance. One afternoon after a long rehearsal for the spring concert, the teacher called for a break. Alicia, her hair in a bouncy ponytail, was talking to her friends. Gaeb walked over to the group and stood behind Alicia, towering over her. She's so small, he thought. He caught their image in the mirror and smiled. Gaeb looked down at Alicia again, then at the oversized T-shirt he was wearing over his undershirt.

"Will she fit?" he whispered. "Yeah, she'll fit." Gaeb nodded, grabbed his T-shirt by the bottom hem, and thrust it over Alicia. It swallowed her all the way down to her thighs.

"Oh, my goodness! Where's Alicia?" Gaeb asked, looking around. Two pairs of legs stuck out from under his shirt.

"Gaeb!" Alicia cried. She laughed in muffled bursts. Gaeb chuckled, and laughter spread throughout the dance studio at the sight of his four-legged T-shirt.

The girl beside Gaeb caught his eye. "Is this your first year at Montgomery College?" she asked.

"Uh-huh. I plan to go on to Maryland State later." Gaeb looked down at his textbook. Sticking out from between the pages was the picture Alicia had taken of him in front of Blake. He was crossed-armed, about seven feet above the ground, having shinnied up between the columns of the school building. Gaeb couldn't believe that only a few months ago he had still been in high school. . . .

Gaeb kept in touch with Alicia after he graduated. Around the middle of the summer she called him to find out how things were going.

"Hey, what's up?" Alicia asked.

He could hear cars in the background. "Where are you? Are you talking and walking?"

"I'm on my way to the pool." Alicia giggled. "I haven't heard from you in a while."

"Lots of rehearsals for the dance company I joined," Gaeb said.

"Great!"

"Nah, I'm quitting."

"Gaeb, I thought joining a company was your dream."

"Uh-huh. But the dudes make fun of me for my jokes."

"What?" Alicia's voice rose. "You want to quit because they think you're funny?"

Maybe he had taken it all wrong. Actually, he liked being funny as much as he liked to dance. Alicia had a point. Gaeb decided to stay on until the season ended.

———

Gaeb glanced at the list of words the professor had written on the chalkboard. Upcoming topics of discussion, the professor said. The word *secrets* stood out. . . .

Alicia was someone who could keep a secret. No matter that you didn't say it was a secret. She knew. She just knew. He told Alicia stuff all the time, things he wouldn't tell most of his guy friends. She was, like, his little sister. Gaeb and Alicia grew closer after she gave him a handmade card for his seventeenth birthday. It fit in the palm of his hand. Inside, Alicia had written all his names in different typefaces: *Gaeb, GNN, Popper, Joker*. It was a really, really nice card. So considerate. He kept the card pinned to a wall in his room. He didn't want to lose it.

When Alicia started going out with Chris, she had asked Gaeb for advice. She trusted him. He trusted her too. Alicia was the person he turned to when he had a situation. There was the time he had liked this girl Taylor. She was real cute. Gaeb couldn't figure out how to get her to notice him. One day at lunch he talked to Alicia about it.

"You know Taylor?" Gaeb asked.

"Yeah, I know her. She's in English with me," Alicia said. "Why? You like her?"

"Uh-huh."

"Okay. Come visit me before third period starts."

So Gaeb showed up at Alicia's English class. He went in the door and without a word sat on Alicia's desk table, staring at the chalkboard. Gaeb figured something funny was sure to get Taylor's attention. She was only two desks away. Alicia started to giggle. Gaeb kept still.

"Gaeb, I can't see." Alicia pulled on his shirt.

"Uh-huh." He could feel Taylor's gaze on him.

"Gaeb!" Alicia raised her voice. "I can't see."

"Oh." Gaeb turned around. "Oh, yeah. Can I borrow your camera?"

"Sure." Alicia pulled her camera out of her green backpack and handed it to Gaeb. As he stood up, he caught Taylor watching him. It had worked. Gaeb glanced at Alicia before leaving. Alicia smiled and nodded. Gaeb and Taylor went out for a while after that.

Yeah. Alicia helped Gaeb, and Gaeb looked out for her. Sometimes Alicia kept things to herself so he wouldn't get mad. Things like Brice. Brice, Travis, and Chris hung out with Gaeb. Gaeb couldn't remember exactly how he'd found out, but he heard that Brice had pushed Alicia. Gaeb was so upset, he wanted to fight the guy. How dare he touch her? Gaeb decided he could no longer be friends with Brice. Alicia meant that much to him.

———

Gaeb felt his cell phone vibrate in his pocket. He slid his hand into his jeans to turn it off. . . .

Gaeb's friend Zena must have called around seven thirty that Saturday morning. Travis had spent the night, and they both had been up early playing video games in Gaeb's room, waiting for the cartoons to come on TV. Gaeb had fallen in love with Saturday morning cartoons when he first came to the United States from Ghana as an eleven-year-old. His favorite was Pokémon.

"Gaeb . . ." Zena hesitated. "You know Alicia?"

"What a stupid question. Of course I know Alicia."

"She was in a car crash last night," Zena blurted out.

Gaeb ended the call without a word. He started pacing the room.

"What happened?" asked Travis, his eyes on the game.

"It's Alicia. She got in a car crash!"

Travis looked at Gaeb blankly and shrugged. "Are you going to keep playing or what?"

"Leave me alone!" Gaeb cried. "Get out of here, man. Now."

Gaeb felt his anger rising: How could Travis be so indifferent? Then a terrible thought occurred to Gaeb. He shut the door behind Travis and called Zena back. She told him Alicia had died. Gaeb hung up again and speed-dialed Alicia's number. No answer. No room for messages. He started to panic. "This can't be! Not Alicia! Not her," he shouted. He slid down along the wall and plunged his head into his hands. He pressed hard against them, like, like . . . wanting to understand why. Why Alicia? Just the week before he had asked her to wish Travis happy birthday at school. That was the last time he'd heard Alicia's voice. He thought of Travis, and his rage welled up again. Just like Brice, Travis didn't understand about Alicia. Gaeb shuddered, his fury suddenly giving way to shock.

Later, at the funeral, Gaeb saw many of Alicia's friends. They were all distraught. He had been to a funeral before, his older half brother's. Gaeb had been very sad, but the grief was nothing like what he felt for Alicia. He was angry too.

Travis hadn't shown. Such disrespect, but somehow Gaeb wasn't surprised.

When Gaeb was leaving the church he bent down to hug Alicia's mother. He felt empty, but he would go on. He had to, death being a part of life and all: You enjoy life while you have it. He and Alicia had shared that for sure.

Cute little Alicia. Like happy, joy, happy . . .

"See you." The girl in Sociology waved at him. Class was over. Gaeb stood and picked up his stuff. He felt a little hungry.

"See you around," Gaeb said with a friendly smile. He walked out of the Social Sciences building and across the courtyard toward the Student Union. Long, slow strides. The day was crisp, sunny, blue. He thought about how good it was that he had stayed on with the dance company through the summer. That working experience had helped him. This fall he had auditioned for a video shoot by a major recording label and had just been picked as a backup dancer. Cool. If everything went right, this December he would be shooting and touring instead of going home to Ghana for the holidays like always.

Damn.

If only Alicia knew.

CHAPTER 6

Kathlynn

Kathlynn couldn't contain herself. She started crying, angry tears burning her cheeks. How could Melissa do this? Even after Kathlynn told her about Alicia dying in a car crash, it was like she didn't get it.

"Yeah, yeah. Don't worry, Kathy," Melissa had said. "Now when I drink I ride with someone else. I know what you're going through."

But that was impossible. Melissa had no idea what Kathlynn was going through. No way. Not even the counselors at school the first week after the accident had known what to say to her. Now, many months later, Kathlynn still didn't want someone who hadn't known Alicia telling her everything was going to be okay when all she wanted was to see her friend again.

If Melissa knew what Kathlynn was feeling she wouldn't party, get drunk, and then ride with a bunch of other drunk kids—all just to be like everybody else. Kathlynn couldn't bear the thought of losing another friend. It gave her chills. She threw her cell phone on her bed and got up to change her T-shirt. Sean was coming over tonight.

A bug flew in front of her. A ladybug that landed on top of her chest of drawers. Alicia! Kathlynn thought, and for a moment a sad smile softened her face. One morning at the beginning of the school year, Kathlynn had been having lunch outside with Alicia when a ladybug landed on their table. "Oh my gosh! I love ladybugs," Alicia cried, sliding a manicured finger next to the tiny bug to lure it onto her hand.

Yes, Alicia had truly liked ladybugs. Kathlynn hadn't realized how much until the week of the funeral, when ladybug stories poured out from Alicia's elementary school friends who were now at Blake.

Ever since she had first seen Alicia in Intermediate Jazz, their dance elective, Kathlynn wanted to be friends with her. Alicia seemed to know everybody, and everyone Kathlynn talked to said how nice Alicia was. The summer before tenth grade they had e-mailed each other a lot. When they ended up on the Poms squad together, they had become good friends.

What Kathlynn missed most was spending time with her friend in the mornings. All during tenth grade they had the same routine. They would both arrive at school around six fifty on one of the early buses. They had lockers across from each other, and after taking out their books for the day they would walk to their meeting spot by the Media Center. They usually had about twenty minutes for "girl talk" before Ben, Sean, Colin, and the others joined them. . . .

"I'm so excited!" Alicia said as she sat on the floor by Kathlynn. "I have leftover sub for lunch."

"Oh, your mom didn't fix you a healthy lunch today?" asked Kathlynn.

"She's on a trip. When she's gone my dad gets pizza or subs for dinner, and we watch the TV shows I love," Alicia explained. "Oh my gosh, Kathlynn, I have to tell you something." Alicia's eyes went wide, and she started rubbing her friend's knee. "You know that boy who keeps following me around?"

"Oh yeah. One of those stalkers, huh?"

"Yeah. His name is Tommy."

"Sure, I know him."

"He follows me in the hallways and tries to hug me."

"Oh, gross. He smells too." Kathlynn screwed up her nose.

"I know. But, anyways, he showed up at my house last Friday afternoon. I wasn't there, but he tells my mom that I had invited him. My mom says he should come back later when I'm home from practice, and he returns at dinnertime. Can you believe it?"

"You didn't invite him, did you?"

"No!"

Kathlynn looked down at her knee and chuckled.

"Why are you laughing?" Alicia asked.

"Why do you keep massaging my knee?"

"Oh, I don't know." Alicia took her hand off Kathlynn's knee and giggled. "You are my girlfriend," Alicia said in a deep voice, raising her left eyebrow. "From now on no one else is allowed to touch your knee." They burst out laughing.

———

The ladybug took flight, then landed on the birthday card Alicia had made for Kathlynn on her sixteenth birthday. . . .

"What do you want for your birthday?" Alicia asked.

"Hey, would you make me a card? Like the one you made for your Poms big sister. It was so cool."

"Yeah, I guess I can."

On her birthday, about twelve of Kathlynn's friends gathered at Harry's Restaurant for her party. Melissa was there; but since she went to a private school, she didn't know most of Kathlynn's friends from Blake. Kathlynn saw that Alicia sat down next to Melissa and was talking with her. That was just like Alicia, making others feel included.

When Kathlynn got around to opening Alicia's present, she went immediately for the card. She took it out of the envelope slowly, making the moment last. It was a square card with bits of pink and yellow tissue paper, dried pansies and leaves, and wavy designs in gel pen. *You will always be my girlfriend*, Alicia had written.

———

Who could have known that half a year later Kathlynn would be the one writing to her friend. Her dead friend . . .

It's been more than three months since you've gone away. I never knew it would be this hard. . . . I hope you like our Poms competition routine in your honor. . . . Oh, and don't worry. Nobody else is allowed to touch my knee! Hee, hee . . . I love you, Alicia. BFF.

Kathlynn slipped the florist's card into its tiny envelope and taped it to the plastic wrapping around the bouquet of flowers. Then she drove to the site of the crash, where a memorial had sprung up right after Alicia's death.

Standing on the shoulder of the road, by the skid marks and bits of greenish glass, Kathlynn stared at what people had left. There were faded flowers at the foot of the telephone pole, and teddy bears, and letters now wrinkled and wet, and a pink cross with hand-painted designs that had started to peel. The school paper's obituary, covered in plastic, was attached to the pole with duct tape. Kathlynn placed her flowers on the pile, as close to the Poms picture as she could get them. In this picture Kathlynn stood right behind Alicia. Because she was so short, Alicia had always been in the front for pictures and routines.

The picture reminded Kathlynn of last summer. She had missed her friend at the front of the kick line during Poms camp. The day Kathlynn got home, Alicia called from her precollege program to find out how the camp training had gone. Kathlynn had been touched that Alicia remembered the date she would return from camp. If anyone remembered, it would be Alicia.

Sean had showed up at Kathlynn's house that afternoon to hang out, but she couldn't stop laughing on the phone with her friend. She had been so happy to hear Alicia's voice. "Tell everybody I say hi," Alicia said before ending the call.

Kathlynn looked at her watch. It was already seven thirty. Melissa must be getting ready to go out to a party—another drinking party where she'd probably get wasted. Kathlynn sighed and wiped her eyes. She had to do something. But what? It was difficult to sort things out. Should she tell her mom? Should she call Melissa's mother? Or would that be wrong?

The doorbell rang, and Kathlynn went downstairs to open the door. It was Sean.

"Hey," he said.

"Hi. Come in."

Sean sat by Kathlynn on the sofa and placed his hand on her knee. "How are you?" he asked.

"Sean, you know you are not allowed to touch my knee," Kathlynn said sweetly, looking into her boyfriend's eyes. No one ever will, she thought. For Alicia.

Suddenly Kathlynn stood up, having made up her mind. "Wait here," she said to Sean. "I have to make a phone call."

CHAPTER 7

Colin

Colin turned on the computer. Fine-tuning the video about Alicia wasn't easy. His video production group had captured all the pictures they had received. Now some stills needed to be shifted. He planned to go into the lab every day of spring break until the video was done. He wanted it ready for the school's Arts Festival. The video would show in the gallery along with Alicia's art. He couldn't wait to see people's reactions to his video. That was how he judged his work.

The Media Production Lab was quiet. Colin paused on a frame. Eighth grade. French class trip to Quebec. That had been right around the time he'd christened Alicia *Little One*. Colin remembered waking up to silly laughter from the back of the charter bus. It was dark outside, and all of the more than thirty kids on the school trip had been asleep—except for Little One and Vicky. Their giggles had been unmistakable. Colin went to see what they were up to. He found the two girls weaving Twizzlers in and out of their hair, making some incredible hairdos. Her hair full of red licorice candy, Little One had been happy, so sweet.

Alicia's happy, sweet nature was what had first drawn Colin to her. He had known Alicia for seven years, since fourth grade; but until her death he hadn't realized how much she meant to him. Yeah. The way he found out was odd, to say the least. . . .

The first weeks after the accident this weird thing happened every school day. Early in the morning Colin found Little One sitting on the floor next to Kathlynn in their regular meeting place before the first-period bell rang. Alicia waved at him, so glad to see him, smiling just like she always had when she was alive. Now, though, he saw her and also saw *through* her. She was like one of those holograms, three-dimensional but transparent. Then Colin saw Alicia four or five more times during the day—in the hallways, at lunch, in class—as often as he used to see her in school before she died.

Visions, that was what the therapist his mom took him to had labeled them. "They'll go away, when you're ready," the therapist said. They did go away, but not for a long while. There was the time Colin was driving to soccer practice. When he looked in his rearview mirror he saw Little One sitting in the backseat, a pink bow in her hair, wearing her Poms jacket and trademark smile. Colin rubbed his eyes, but she was still there. A hologram. The car in front of him swerved, and Colin increased his distance from it.

———

Thinking back to that incident, Colin realized he had become more cautious when he drove. He was more aware of other drivers and how they behaved on the road. Before that Friday last September, he used to think that nothing bad could happen to someone young and healthy like himself. Colin didn't think that anymore. How could he, after what had happened to Alicia? She had gotten into a car with a kid who lost control just six days after Colin had driven with her for the first, and only, time. . . .

Early on Saturday afternoon Colin drove to Alicia's house. Sean was in the van with him. They were picking up Alicia to go to the movies in downtown Silver Spring. When Colin rang the doorbell, Alicia's father greeted him. Colin remembered him from her birthday parties.

"So, how long have you been driving, Colin?" Alicia's father asked.

"*Ahem.*" Colin put his hands in his pockets. "About seven months now, sir."

"Well, be careful on the road." Her father looked out to check the van parked in the driveway.

As Colin and Alicia turned to go, her mother stepped onto

the porch. "You're just going to the movies, right?" she asked.

"*Sí*, Mami. Yes. Bye, Mami! Bye, Papi!" Alicia flashed a smile at her parents before jumping into the van behind the driver's seat. "You know, you are two of the first friends my parents have let me ride with," she said. She caught Colin's eye in the rearview mirror and smiled at him.

"Wait! You forgot to tell me your blood type," Alicia's father teased as they pulled out of the driveway.

Colin looked at the computer screen. Back to the introduction. The shots zoomed in and out in black-and-white. Words Alicia's friends had come up with scrolled slowly across the screen from left to right in white type: *Caring, Loving, Inspirational, Fun* . . . Yeah. She was fun. Colin leaned back in the chair and rested his head in the palms of his hands. He gazed into the distance. . . .

Only a few weeks ago, right before lunch, Colin was standing in front of the cafeteria next to a group of eleventh-grade girls. He liked one of them very much. Should he approach her? he wondered. Would he have a chance? Suddenly he heard Alicia's easy laugh announcing her arrival. He saw her and Amanda walking toward him. This was his opportunity to get some advice. He had asked for it many times.

"Hey, Little One!" Colin called.

Alicia locked her eyes on his. Colin nodded toward the girl in question. Alicia looked at her and then back at Colin. She frowned and raised her left eyebrow. That gave him the answer. Colin knew exactly what Alicia's gestures meant: Don't even try. Colin sighed, but he knew Little One was probably right. The girl was out of his league. He smiled at Alicia. How he loved their unspoken language.

———

Colin turned up the video's volume. He liked the music his production group had chosen to accompany the section called "Alicia the Dancer." It went well with the pictures of the Poms squad winning the county competition for its division. Alicia had loved Poms. One day in May of ninth grade she had asked for his opinion. . . .

"Hi. You want to take a walk?"

"Sure," Colin said. Every so often they would take these walks during lunch period and unload what was on their minds.

"I'm not staying with ballet," Alicia began. As they walked down the hall she greeted all the people she knew, her hands fluttering this way and that. "And, I don't think the dance program here is that strong. So I don't know if I want to take dance classes in school."

"So what are you going to do?"

"I don't know." Alicia hesitated for a moment. "Should I join Poms?"

"You can try it out for a year and see if you like it," Colin suggested.

"Yeah!" Alicia looked at him, her eyes sparkling.

Later, Colin was sure he had never seen Alicia as excited as she was that morning in tenth grade when she told him she made the Poms squad. He knew dance was part of who she was.

———

Colin had gotten the idea to make the video on the afternoon he and Ben were getting ready to go to the crash site. Ben had been printing out the poem he had written for Alicia, and he asked Colin if he wanted to sign it. He could have, but it wasn't his poem. Colin wasn't good at writing poetry. His talent was producing videos.

He picked up the script he had written for the video. It was called *A Community Remembers*. Everyone had pretty much stuck to his script during the recording. "Alicia the Friend," the closing section, was playing. "If you had to describe Alicia in one word, what would you say?" That had been the prompt for the kids interviewed, and everyone had gone on to say much more.

Tristan's words came last, voicing over the only close-up clip of Alicia that anybody had—the one shot at Julia's sixteenth birthday party. It showed Alicia with a brilliant smile, turning slowly toward the camera.

Tristan's voice was deep and clear, filled with emotion.

"I've said it before, Alicia was an angel out of place . . ."

Colin was glad to have made the video.

". . . one of the most amazing people I've ever experienced."

His video had already made some people weep.

"She was something you wanted to strive to become . . ."

It would be a lasting gift for his friends to remember Alicia.

". . . just a genuinely great person."

Little One.

Fade to black.

CHAPTER 8

Lauren

At eleven twenty-seven on that awful Friday evening, Lauren started to sob. She knew the exact time because she looked at the clock on the microwave when she went into the kitchen for a glass of water. What she didn't know was why she was crying.

Lauren had been watching a movie with her boyfriend, Stefano. They were in such a good mood, laughing and all. Usually she left Stefano's house by ten forty-five, but on this night she had called her mother to ask if she could stay until the movie was over. Her mom agreed.

Lauren's sobs were relentless, almost uncontrollable.

"What's the matter?" Stefano asked when Lauren returned to the living room. "What's wrong?"

"I don't know." Lauren slumped onto the sofa, bawling.

A little while later Lauren was driving home, her green eyes red from so much crying. The night was starless and quiet, the roads completely empty. As empty as she felt. Hollow. But why did she feel this way?

It wasn't until months later, when Lauren heard Alicia's father talk at a safe teen driving workshop, that she learned the actual time of her friend's death: eleven twenty-seven. She had been that connected.

And now?

Lauren picked up the ladybug dilly head-boppers that were propped against the lamp on her nightstand. The headband looked like an insect's antennae. Lauren stroked the feathery green balls where the ladybugs sat. Alicia's *quinceañera* had been so much fun. Fifteen was a very special age for Puerto Rican girls, Alicia had explained. Her mother had wanted Alicia to have a big party to celebrate her *quince*, with music and dancing; but Alicia decided to go with a sleepover instead. That was why the girls had ended up in connecting rooms at the Hyatt hotel in Baltimore's Inner Harbor. Alicia's parents had been in a room a few doors down the hall.

Lauren had never been invited to a *quinceañera* before. She still had the invitation—a small, pink daisy that pulled out of a paper jeans pocket. Alicia had handwritten all the information. . . .

The whole thing was going to be a little weird, Lauren thought. She was the only one from their middle school group of friends who was at Paint Branch High. She kept in touch with Alicia and Cameron, but she hadn't talked to Jodi, Kate, Corrina, Natalie, or Vicky in, like, forever. Definitely—it was going to be weird.

Lauren's fear dissolved on the way down to the hotel lobby. She, Alicia, and Vicky were in the glass elevator, all wearing jeans and snug tops, clutching small handbags under their arms.

"So, you have to tell me," Vicky said, looking at Alicia with big brown eyes. "What's going on with Chris?"

"Oh, you don't want to hear about that scumbag," Lauren said, sweeping back her long, blonde hair. Alicia had told Lauren about her on-and-off relationship with Chris. "Alicia gets mad when Chris spends his lunchtime smoking."

"It's not that bad." Alicia fixed her wispy bangs. "Once he quit for two weeks, just for me."

"Ahhhh," said Vicky.

"Anyways, I'm sort of going out with his friend Chad."

"Shut up!" Vicky's jaw dropped. "Chad is Chris's best friend, right? Alicia, don't tell me your parents don't know about this boyfriend either."

"Nah." Alicia giggled. "They still think I'm too young to have a boyfriend. I'm working on it, though."

"Yeah, yeah. I bet they think you're going to fall for the wrong guy or something," said Vicky.

"At least I introduced Chad to my mom the other day when she picked me up."

"You're too much!" Vicky exclaimed.

Lauren looked from Vicky to Alicia. Suddenly she realized things felt just the way they used to back in middle school. Alicia hadn't changed at all. They all talked to her, so through her everyone was still connected. Yeah.

At the Tex-Mex restaurant, Cameron gave Alicia a bag full of ladybug things, just as she had for every one of Alicia's birthdays since sixth grade. In it were the ladybug dilly boppers. Alicia thought the dilly boppers were so cute that she wore them the entire evening at the restaurant. She wore them in the hotel room when the surprise cake arrived and they sang happy birthday in English and Spanish. She wore them when she changed into the skimpy striped shorts and aqua shirt that were her pajamas. She was still wearing the dilly boppers when, being totally silly, she fell from the bed and ended up crammed between the mattress and the wall. With her legs propped up on the top of the bed, Alicia wiggled her toes to show off the five different shades of pastel nail polish she had painted on them. The girls laughed so hard. Then Vicky couldn't resist. She slid down the wall next to Alicia. Kate joined them next, followed by Natalie, Jody, and finally Lauren. Cameron was busy taking pictures and recording every hilarious instant for her scrapbook: a row of girls, a row of legs, a row of feet and toes. They hardly slept that night, goofing around with one another, talking about school and boys, and drinking sparkling apple cider as if it were champagne.

After brunch the next morning they all went out for a walk before Alicia's parents drove them home. Alicia made everyone lock arms on the pedestrian bridge overlooking the harbor. It was cloudy and on the chilly side for the first weekend in May, but they skipped and laughed and made lots of people stare at them. Just like old times.

Lauren was amazed at how Alicia had brought everyone together. The next day she called her friend. "Wow!" Lauren said. "You did, like, such a good job with it."

"I know!" Alicia said.

———

Lauren put down the dilly boppers. Not too long ago she had found them in Alicia's room, and Alicia's mom let her have them. Lauren kept visiting Alicia's parents, half expecting to see her friend again. But she never did. She wondered where Alicia could have gone. Lauren had seen the casket at the funeral, but she couldn't believe that Alicia was buried in some cemetery. Her smile wasn't buried. Her attitude wasn't buried. She was too gorgeous, too well put together, too herself. Tears filled Lauren's eyes. . . .

After that huge fight she had with Stefano at the end of tenth grade, Lauren was furious. She poured out her feelings to Alicia in one of those long voice mail messages they left on each other's cell phones almost every day, full of the nitty-gritty of their love lives.

Then one afternoon Alicia called.

"Hey, guess who I saw at the Blake thing?" she said. "You know, the dance recital."

"Who?" Lauren asked.

"Stefano."

"You didn't say hi, did you?"

"Actually . . . I did."

"What!" Lauren yelled. "You should have ignored him."

"I was really nice to him," Alicia said. "Sorry."

"You are incredible!" Lauren blurted out, laughing.

The following September Lauren and Stefano got back together, and Stefano told Lauren what had happened. He had been talking with friends during the intermission at the recital when all of a sudden he saw Alicia looking at him. He expected her to turn around and walk the other way, but instead she came up to talk with him. Of all Lauren's friends, Stefano said he liked Alicia best.

Through her bedroom window Lauren could see the sun beginning to set. The sky was turning deep orange, pink, purple. Unreal colors. Alicia's colors. Alicia's painting it! Lauren thought.

Lauren used to be so spiritual. She used to believe she and every other person had a purpose in life, a God-given purpose. Not anymore. When Lauren thought about what had happened to Alicia, how could she believe? It didn't make sense that her friend was gone. She ached for Alicia. In her last voice mail Alicia had listed the guys with whom she could go to homecoming. Then, because the memory on her cell phone was almost full, Lauren did something she rarely did. She deleted her friend's message. Now Lauren could kick herself. She would have loved to replay Alicia's message every day. Was she not supposed to have the message? Why? They had talked, like, two or three times a week. No matter what else was happening, they always knew what was going on in each other's lives. Wasn't it because she was so connected to Alicia that out of the blue she had burst into sobs at the exact moment her friend died? Why had she lost that connection? Lauren had written letters to Alicia, but were the words reaching her? Where was Alicia? Where was her spirit? Lauren was scared to believe in heaven now. She didn't want to be wrong about its existence. If Alicia still was, still existed, why didn't Lauren know? Had Alicia forgotten her? There was, like, a big wall between them. The Wall. It was better to think there was nothing after you die. Nothing.

And still.

Back in April Lauren had dreamed she was in a ballet studio with Alicia. There were other people present, but it was Alicia she remembered. Alicia looked exactly as she had in real life, from her nails to her face to the way she did her hair. She had been so happy. Lauren talked to her. It had all been so vivid, so bright and clear. Lauren had woken up with the feeling that Alicia wasn't gone. She felt as if she had visited with her friend once again. Lauren felt good, just as she felt when she used to talk to Alicia on the phone. Was it real? Was it normal? she wondered. If Alicia was trying to contact Lauren, Lauren should believe. But she couldn't.

The Wall.

How she wished it would crumble.

CHAPTER 9

Vikki

A year after Alicia's death Vikki would say the Saturday of the HFStival was one of the best days of her life. . . .

It was early afternoon on a hot spring Saturday that felt like summer. The stadium was full, although not as packed as it would be later in the day. Vikki was wearing jeans with a belt and hat that matched her pink tank top. The hat was Matt's idea. He had been to many outdoor rock concerts and warned Vikki and Alicia about the sun. Alicia didn't do the hat thing. Instead, she applied sunscreen to her face and wore her hair in long, thinly braided cornrows to keep cool. She had on loose burgundy track pants and a T-shirt, with her bikini top underneath.

Vikki and Alicia had planned to attend the annual HFStival

rock concert for weeks. They couldn't wait to see some of the twenty bands that were on the roster. Vikki had been surprised that Alicia liked the same music she did. She kept finding out new things about her friend all the time.

They had traveled to the stadium by Metro, with Alicia's dad. Vikki thought it was kind of cool that he wanted to see The Cure. It had been the final band announced on the FM radio station 99.1 WHFS, and it was scheduled to play last. Most of their friends were coming by themselves, though.

"Hey, let's get closer," Alicia said, grabbing Vikki by the arm. "Oh my gosh! Let's hurry. That's Yellowcard onstage! My favorite band!"

Vikki already knew how much Alicia liked Yellowcard. Once, during lunch, they had been talking about the concert and some boys had made fun of Alicia for liking Yellowcard. They thought the band wasn't great. "You know what?" Alicia had said, "I don't care. I like them."

Alicia led the way as the girls snaked through the crowd. For a while Alicia's father followed, far behind. Vikki saw how easily her petite friend squeezed her way to the front. But her small size also made it hard for Alicia to see the stage—until she spotted Chris. Vikki knew about Chris. She thought it was amazing that Alicia could find common ground with all sorts of people, from those who were shy to those who were crazy and wild. Chris was a wild one. He was very tall too.

"Hi," Alicia called, coming up behind Chris. "This is my friend Vikki. Hey, would you lift me up so I can see better?"

"Sure," Chris said, and hoisted Alicia. She sat on his shoulders, beaming. She knew every Yellowcard song by heart, and she belted out the songs with the band for the whole set. As soon as it was over, Alicia climbed down, thanked Chris, and turned to go. They needed to go for a walk, Alicia said to Vikki, so they could find their friends.

The sun burned down on the girls, and they craved a drink of water. They pushed their way out of the stadium and into the lot where the concession stands were supposed to be. They passed the body-piercing stands and beer booths. High above, helicopters hovered in the cloudless sky.

"What are you doing this summer?" Alicia asked, fanning herself with her concert program. She slipped the program into her pants pocket, then stripped down to her bikini top and tied her T-shirt around her waist.

"I'll be at Peabody." Vikki was into music, and the Peabody Institute in Baltimore was one of the best places in the country to study music. Vikki played drums, marimba, and piano. She had told Alicia about the amount of practice her instruments required. "I guess I'm going to do more with music when I graduate. Music and psychology, I think."

"That's so cool!" Alicia exclaimed.

you in?

Vikki loved that she could talk about college with Alicia. In tenth grade none of her other friends were interested. They would have said she was a nerd if she brought it up. Vikki supposed she was a nerd, being in honors classes and always having her nose in psychology books. Alicia was different. She was spunky, crazy, and fun, but also smart and competitive. The first time Vikki had noticed her was in French class. Everyone went to Alicia for help because she was so good.

"And what are you doing?" Vikki asked. She was looking at her concert program, trying to figure out a way through the sea of people to a stand that sold water.

"I'm doing this precollege program to build up my art portfolio. They say RISD is hard to get into."

"You already know where you want to go?" Vikki asked.

"Yeah. It's this school in Providence—the Rhode Island School of Design. It's right next to Brown."

"Providence! That's where my grandparents live," Vikki exclaimed.

"Hey," Alicia said. "If I get lonely I'll go visit them."

"Okay." Vikki smiled. It would be so funny if Alicia showed up at her grandparents' house just like that.

When they finally got to the water stand the girls stood staring at the little bottles priced at five dollars each. There had to be some cheaper water nearby. Vikki and Alicia continued on in search of it. Soon they ran into Tyler. He joined them.

"Look, a hose!" Alicia picked it up, ready to drink.

"Are you crazy?" Tyler yanked the hose away. "Haven't you heard about the lead in D.C.'s water?"

"Who cares?" said Alicia.

"We're thirsty," Vikki said. "We want water!"

"Oh yeah?" Tyler raised the hose and gleefully sprayed them. The water cooled their burning skin. Vikki saw that Alicia had closed her eyes and opened her mouth wide as she tried to catch the stream of water without choking. They were laughing so much, it was hard to drink.

Later in the day the girls bumped into Daniel. Poor Daniel, he looked as if he was going to pass out. He told them he had lost his wallet and wasn't able to buy anything to drink. Dehydrated, Vikki diagnosed. They needed to help him right away. So they bought him one of those expensive little bottles of water and saved his life. At least that's what Daniel said when he thanked them.

A little before dusk Vikki and Alicia found where the bands' tour buses were parked. They ran to the buses when they saw some band members walking across the lot. Alicia managed to get an autograph from the lead singer of the Lostprophets. She even got Vikki to take her picture with him. Later, Alicia kept talking about how good-looking he was and his cute British accent.

––––––––––––

Vikki put down her marimba mallets. She rubbed her temples. Sometimes thinking about when—and if—her friends would get over Alicia's death gave her a headache. . . .

That first week after the accident, Vikki was worried about Daniel. He was a mess and needed to talk to someone, so she accompanied him to the counselor. In the office they met this boy, George. He was beside himself, crying for Alicia as if he had lost his best friend. Neither Vikki nor Daniel had ever heard of him, so Vikki asked George how he knew Alicia. George told her that Alicia would help him in physics with the problems the teacher assigned. Alicia would always try to make conversation. Not many people did that for him. Not many people would give him the time of day. Vikki listened to George and wept with him.

That entire first month was horrible. Vikki's group of friends was falling apart. Amanda announced that she wasn't going to sit with her and Kathlynn at lunch anymore because it was too painful. Then Kathlynn became angry, and Vikki guessed Kathlynn felt that she had now lost two friends. Vikki wanted to console her friends, but she really didn't know how. Were all these reactions normal? She had to find out.

One day while browsing the psychology section at the public library Vikki found some books with personal stories about grief. She checked out the books and read them at home until she could read no more. She figured she would be patient. She wanted to help people. She just needed to listen.

Vikki closed her music book. She thought about how her feelings had changed with time. A few days before the accident one of her friends had commented that Vikki hadn't been hanging out with Alicia as much as she had in tenth grade. Vikki told her friend that she and Alicia didn't have classes together, but they had all of eleventh grade to spend time with each other at lunch and after school. After the accident, Vikki wished she had done something right away to see more of Alicia. She had missed her chance.

Still, Vikki felt blessed to have known Alicia. Vikki was trying to live her life a little more like her friend. She tried to have a good time in all situations. She had seen how important it was to listen and help others deal with stuff. Above all, when Vikki saw a relationship falling apart, she refused to let it happen. She would say to her friends, "Do something about it!"

And she followed that advice by taking care of her own friendships.

CHAPTER 10

Ben sat on the worn green couch, cradling his acoustic guitar. He had dimmed the basement lights and lit some candles to create the right mood. He played a few chords. His Adam's apple quivered as he sang.

"A rose flitters through this September night
I miss your eyes twinkling in the twilight"

The words flowed freely, as they had the day he composed the ballad months before. He had been so surprised back then at how the words popped into his mind one after the other in an uninterrupted chain. He never had to rewrite them. It had paid off to wait a month after Alicia's death for the rawness of his feelings to subside and for his life to recover a sense of reality.

Ben thought about how people have different traits and

different ways to make you feel better. Alicia's special trait had been her smile. She would just smile at you with that twinkle in her eyes and change your mood to align with hers. Quite a trick.

Alicia's trick had helped Ben back in ninth grade. He suffered from depression; and when he was down, there were very few people he could talk to. Alicia had been one of them. She would look at him with that smile on her face and tell him nice things until he came out of his sadness. She would talk about what he was good at. She never talked about herself. So it wasn't surprising that it took until the end of tenth grade for Ben to find out about Alicia's artistic talent. . . .

They had an English assignment to write about how they had changed in the past year. Alicia jazzed up her essay with drawings and magazine cutouts. It was incredible.

"That's so neat!" Ben said, looking over his shoulder at the homework papers Mr. Potyk had just handed back to Alicia.

"Thanks." Alicia giggled, and put away her work.

"You never told me you were an artist."

"Yeah, well . . ." Alicia smiled. "Hey, what else have you written after the 'Porcelain' poem? That one was so beautiful."

"Don't change the subject. How long have you been doing that kind of stuff?" Ben demanded, raising his voice. "What else do you have?"

"Oh, nothing. Shhh!" Alicia pointed to the teacher. "Pay attention."

He had to give up. Alicia was too much trouble sometimes, not wanting to answer his questions or talk about herself.

———

Ben closed his eyes and tilted his head to one side. He ran his long, thin fingers over the guitar strings. The wisps of smoke from a burnt-out candle swirled next to him. His voice became higher.

"And now I know you're inside of me
Waiting but grasping me endlessly
I look to see your face inside the clouds
More perfect,
more perfect than ever could be"

A chuckle rose in Ben's throat. He loved Alicia's funny faces. At lunch her faces had made everyone at the table roar with laughter. She had this one face where she crossed her eyes and then made them move independently of each other in wide circles. It made some of the girls squirm and beg her to stop. Alicia would always crack up afterward. The silly faces and the burping contests she competed in showed everyone how down-to-earth and real Alicia was. . . .

The Friday she died, Ben and Alicia had eaten lunch together.

"You know I ride my bike a lot around your neighborhood," he said.

"Really?" Alicia brightened. "Why don't you come over sometime this weekend, and we can hang out?"

"Yeah," Ben said. He made a mental note to do just that. It would be fun to ride over and spend time with her.

Later that evening Ben and a bunch of his friends decided to go to their favorite restaurant. They talked about inviting girls, including Alicia; but in the end they all agreed it was going to be a guys' night out.

Afterward, Ben couldn't help thinking that if they had asked Alicia to come along she might still be alive. Over and over he thought about the driver of the car. This kid and his reckless driving had deprived him and so many others of Alicia. Ben's blood would rise and his skin burn with resentment. On the other hand, he feared that when the kid returned to school, he would be beaten up. Ben didn't want that either. Much later he heard that the driver of the car was back at the wheel. Ben's hope that the kid's license would be revoked was shattered.

So many feelings to unravel.

———————

"My tears have dried for I'm comforted
Because now you grace the angels with your
your beautiful smile"

Since Alicia died, Ben often felt her presence. He felt it on the baseball field when, after a long, dry spell, he managed to hit the ball a lot harder than he had in a long time. He felt it when he was so scared about the sudden sharp pain in his chest. He was soothed by Alicia's voice in his head telling him he would be okay.

"Here I go leaving inside of you
Letting go there's nothing left to do
And I look to see your face inside the clouds"
And Ben had felt Alicia's presence when she saved his life. . . .

On the night before the fund-raising race at school, Ben was driving home after several hours of band practice. His band was going to play at the event the next morning. It was raining and Ben was tired. He made a hard left turn onto a country road and was immediately confronted by a car driving on the wrong side of the road, approaching fast. Ben swerved, skidded, and lost control of the car. In an instant he broke out in a cold sweat. His mouth went dry. A million thoughts crowded his mind. But then he heard Alicia's voice deep within him. *Calm down.* Her words centered him. *Don't go crazy. Think. Get back on the road.* Ben gained control of the car and inched forward to the nearest place where he could pull over—a church's parking lot. As his car came to a stop, Ben collapsed, crying, relieved, thankful.

"Your memory cherished, your work never done"
Ben's voice became a whisper.

"Yet it has begun
We carry the tools inside our hearts
To complete this imperfect world—
and become one with your image."

You really don't know how much time you are going to have, Ben now knew. Alicia had been a great person, and he was trying to be more like her—more compassionate, tolerant, and joyful. He was striving for perfection, because Alicia would have accepted nothing less. Colin called her Little One. For one so little, she had a lot to give. Even now, Ben realized, whenever he felt anxious, thinking of Alicia calmed him and lifted his spirits.

"And now I know you're inside of me . . ."

CHAPTER 11

Vicky

It was the little things that Vicky remembered. . . .

During the summer before their sophomore year of high school, Vicky and Alicia had met for dinner at Bethesda Row. Known for the boutiques, theaters, and restaurants lining the streets, the area was often full of kids from nearby high schools. The girls sat across from each other at the restaurant on the corner of Woodmont Avenue, digging their spoons into the large scoops of vanilla ice cream melting over the warm, double-size brownie. Multicolored sprinkles ran down the brownie's thick, chocolate sides and collected in the pool of ice cream at the bottom of the plate. Having a scrumptious dessert for dinner was something they relished. It was really, really good.

After being so close in middle school, Vicky and Alicia now attended different high schools. Their friendship had become a long-distance kind of thing. They saw each other only once or twice a year, but Alicia was still one of Vicky's best friends. It was pretty cool.

They had so much in common. They had laughed until they cried that day in sixth grade when they discovered the coincidences. Both were Hispanic. Both had older sisters named Verónica who were in the same grade at the same high school. Both of their mothers had the same nickname. They immediately felt a bond.

Their dinner finished, Vicky and Alicia went into the theater next door to see *Spellbound*. Less than halfway through the movie Alicia started mumbling.

"What is it?" whispered Vicky.

"Mmm."

"What?" Vicky whispered louder.

"Mmmmmm . . ."

"What?" insisted Vicky. "What?"

"This is really boring," Alicia said. "Let's go get some Twizzlers."

"Shhh!" someone hissed from behind.

Out in the lobby, a blond boy was standing behind the candy counter.

"How much are the Twizzlers?" Vicky asked.

"Four dollars."

"Oh! That's SO expensive," the girls exclaimed in unison.

"What's your name?" Alicia leaned on the counter.

"Gregg."

"So, how much for the Twizzlers, Gregg?" Vicky said, placing her arm over Alicia's shoulders. "Remember, we're students."

"Okay. Three."

"For this size candy?" Alicia pleaded with her eyes.

"Okay. Take it," Gregg muttered. "Give me a dollar, but don't tell anybody."

"We won't!" the girls promised.

––––––

Natalie elbowed Vicky at the grave site. "So? Are you going to translate what it says?"

Today was the one-year anniversary. Family and friends had gathered at the old cemetery for the blessing of the headstone. Vicky felt sick to her stomach. On a sunny Saturday like this a year ago, Vicky, her parents, and her brother had been up early, getting ready to leave for Family Day at her sister's college in Pennsylvania. Vicky had been eating breakfast when her mother came into the kitchen weeping to give her the news. She hugged Vicky and kept repeating, "I don't know what I would do if it were my daughter. It's just awful, just awful!" They had gone to Pennsylvania that day; and while the other families had a good time, Vicky couldn't stop having flashbacks, remembering the quirky adventures and silly times of years past. She had cried in front of everyone as she remembered the little things. Like now.

Vicky laughed softly and licked away a salty tear. Seventh grade. Eastern Middle School. The Riqui thing . . .

"If I don't come back or something, or if I'm taking a really long time, you come and get me," Alicia said. She smoothed her lip gloss with her thumb and index finger, then stared into Vicky's eyes. "We're meeting on the staircase by the Foreign Language Lab."

"Yeah, yeah. If you don't come back in, like, whatever, I come and get you." Funny how Alicia always had a plan of action. Vicky saw Alicia ask Ms. Ski for a bathroom pass and leave Media, the communications class.

Vicky followed through. She actually went to get her friend once she thought too much time had elapsed. Vicky thought Riqui was kind of shady. He was in eighth grade, and the excitement of going with an older boy appealed to Alicia. She also loved how he called her *mi princesa*. Alicia had never been anyone's princess before.

Even later, in high school, Riqui was still infatuated with Alicia. He would wait for her outside school near the buses. Alicia always dragged Vicky along to these meetings, never quite sure she wanted to be alone with him. Vicky knew her presence gave Alicia an excuse to leave at any time. Always in control. Always with a plan.

———

"Vicky . . . ," Natalie insisted.

Vicky tried to focus through her tears. She read the poem engraved on the back of the white marble headstone to herself, pausing after each verse.

Pues se fue la niña bella,
bajo el cielo y sobre el mar,
a cortar la blanca estrella
que la hacía suspirar.

It was difficult to translate, even harder to speak. Alicia's parents arrived, and the same priest from the funeral mass led the group in prayer. Vicky and Natalie moved to one side. Chad, Corrina, and Colin were standing right across from them.

Looking at Colin, Vicky recalled how a year ago he had told her that Alicia wanted to hang out with her soon. And that Friday evening, just a few hours before she died, Alicia had told Vicky the same thing. By chance they had both been online, instant-messaging. Weird, because neither of them went online much. Instead, they called each other on their cell phones and left long voice messages. Now, Vicky thought of that coincidence as a sign. Alicia was saying good-bye or something. Alicia was thinking of her.

Alicia's mother thanked everybody for coming and explained why the headstone had taken so long. It had been difficult to find a sculptor for the relief portrait of Alicia that was carved on the front of the stone. It's so pretty, Vicky thought. Alicia's mother translated the verses of Rubén Darío, the Nicaraguan poet.

"So the beautiful girl left,
under the sky and above the sea,
to clip the bright white star
that made her always sigh."

Vicky was suddenly relieved. She knew Natalie would understand now. . . .

For Vicky, being in a different school when Alicia died was both hard and easy. Hard because nobody understood what Vicky was feeling. She was so sad. She cried for four days in a row, almost without a break. The English teacher sent Vicky to the school counselor, but not even the counselor could help her. Vicky didn't know what to tell herself. She didn't know what to do with her sadness. Natalie didn't want to talk about Alicia or how she felt, and none of her other friends had known Alicia well enough.

Eventually Vicky discovered a way to move on, a way that helped her stop crying and cope. She didn't want to forget Alicia, but she didn't want to dwell on her death either. She didn't want to be a crybaby all the time. Since they hadn't seen each other much after they started high school, Vicky began to think they had just lost touch. It was as if Alicia were out there somewhere living her life, and they just didn't talk anymore. That was how Vicky dealt with the loss of her friend for almost a year. It had made it easy. Well, easier.

Alicia's parents invited everybody to their home to share some of Alicia's favorite foods. Vicky and Natalie rode together to Alicia's house. In the kitchen, Alicia's mother was frying some *surullitos de maiz,* steam rising from the pile of corn fritters. People were streaming into the dining room to get something to eat. There were tiny egg salad sandwiches, fried ham-and-cheese sandwiches, lemon squares, and brownies.

"No Pop-Tarts," Colin said, knowing it would make Vicky smile.

It did. The little things . . .

Early one morning in seventh grade, before first period, Alicia and Vicky were in front of their lockers.

"Do you have any money?" Alicia asked. She fumbled in her backpack, searching for coins. She found a quarter.

"For a Pop-Tart?" Vicky loved the jam-filled toaster pastries as much as her friend. She looked in every corner of her locker. She came up with forty cents.

"Not enough." Alicia sighed.

"Wait, wait." Vicky forced her hand into her jeans pocket and found another quarter. "Here!"

"Yea!" Alicia said. They high-fived and raced to the vending machine to get their favorite, a frosted strawberry Pop-Tart. Neither Vicky nor Alicia could get Pop-Tarts at home. Their moms didn't like junk food. It was so annoying.

Alicia unwrapped the Pop-Tart eagerly, licking her lips. She was about to break it in two when a kid bumped into her.

"Oh no!" Vicky and Alicia screamed as the pastry fell on the dingy linoleum floor.

Then a boy walking by kicked the Pop-Tart, sending it far down the hallway. Vicky and Alicia ran to pick it up. They looked at each other.

"It's, like, ninety cents," Alicia said, raising an eyebrow.

"Hey." Vicky grinned.

They ate it.

———

All of Alicia's friends were in her room. The room was still sponge-painted pink and had two walls covered with cutouts from teen magazines. Strings of cutout circles hung from the ceiling and swayed when people moved around. It felt so nice in there. It was all about Alicia. Her mom had said they could each choose something of Alicia's for themselves. Vicky looked in the many little boxes Alicia had kept on her nightstand and found two identical silver bracelets. She took one for herself and handed the other one to Natalie. She hoped Natalie would open up after today. It would be good for Natalie to talk about how she felt.

Vicky slipped the bracelet over her wrist. Wearing it would be a way to remember Alicia. She lingered behind as the others left, then turned around to look into the room once more. She thought about how many times Alicia had called her from here, probably sitting on the carpet right in front of the wall mirrors, staring at herself.

They would always end their conversations with an "I love you" kind of thing:

"You're awesome, Alicia."

"You're the best, Vicky."

It was the little things. Vicky smiled.

CHAPTER 12

Madison

"Hey, let's call Alicia!" Jessie fumbled in her bag for her cell phone. "Is that okay?"

"Sure!" Madison adjusted the seat of her lawn chair. It would be great to catch up with her former playdate pal. She couldn't wait to see her. Madison, Alicia, and Jessie, as well as Julia, Megan, Kathryn, and Heather, had been Brownie Girl Scouts together. They had gone to one another's birthday parties. They were the Stonegate Elementary girls.

Madison had been so busy during the summer that she had hardly seen any of her former classmates. Sitting next to Jessie at the top of the hill by the neighborhood pool, she could look down on everything—the lifeguards, the pool's entrance, the parking lot.

After just twenty minutes, the time it had taken Alicia to walk to the pool, Madison saw her friend come through the gate. Alicia chatted with the kids in the lifeguards' office by the entrance. Then she joked with Kyle, who was on lifeguard duty up in the chair at the shallow end of the pool. Finally Alicia approached them, waving excitedly. She looked cute in her red, bandana-print tank top and shorts.

"Hey!" Alicia called. She hugged Madison, then flashed a big smile. "What's going on with you?"

"Everything's good."

"But tell me! How's school?" Alicia insisted. After ninth grade at Blake, Madison had gone to boarding school in Virginia. Now Madison found it difficult to come back home and be reminded by friends of how things had changed, of what she had missed. She felt some people kind of wanted to know what she'd been doing, but they kind of didn't really care. With Alicia, things were different. Madison never felt awkward around her. She never felt left out. Alicia was her same sweet self, just like from their days at Stonegate.

"It's okay. I like my photography class a lot," Madison said.

"Any boyfriends?" Alicia looked directly into Madison's eyes.

"Well, yeah. There's this boy, Sam. You would like him." Madison heard her raspy voice reach a smooth, high pitch when talking about her boyfriend. She revealed every detail of their relationship in long, run-on sentences. She couldn't help herself. Alicia looked so intensely interested.

"Hey, Alicia, where's your bathing suit?" Jessie interrupted.

"Oh, I have driving school in a little while."

"You promised me and Julia that you would get into the pool by the end of the summer," Jessie reminded her friend.

"Yeah, well, the water is way too cold. Anyways, summer will be over soon." Alicia sat next to Madison. "I can't wait for school to start to see everybody again."

Madison and Jessie looked at each other. Suddenly the girls heard rolling skateboards nearing the pool entrance. They went down to talk to the skater boys. After a while Alicia had to leave, and Madison and Jessie went back up to the chairs on the hill.

"She has a zillion friends. I don't know how she does it," Madison said. "Do you remember in ninth grade how she'd go up to all kinds of people and make friends with them?"

"I know. It's like Julia says. Alicia migrates and picks up friends wherever she goes. She eats her lunch in five minutes and then starts walking around and talking to people. She's so goofy." Jessie laughed. "She makes everything, like, funny, easy. At lunch if there's an awkward silence, she makes a silly face to end it, or she thinks of something to say."

"Yeah," Madison said, nodding.

"There isn't anyone who doesn't like her. She's Alicia."

"She's so genuine and everything." Madison looked down. "Not a lot of people are that way," she whispered.

A year and a half later on an unseasonably mild winter day, Madison was walking her black Labrador retriever by the pool. She thought of that lazy summer afternoon. It was the last time Madison had seen her childhood friend. She had met Alicia at recess in first grade. Some kids had been playing at being dogs. They needed a mom dog, and they asked Madison to be it. Jessie, Julia, Megan, Alicia, Alex, and Kevin had been the puppies; Scott the dad dog. They played dogs every day for that entire year.

One day after playing dogs Alex started squashing ladybugs in front of Alicia. He knew she liked them. Alicia got so upset, she chased Alex all around the playground, waving her little arms and screaming, "Don't crush the ladybugs! Don't crush the ladybugs!" Later, Jessie told Madison she thought that incident might have been the beginning of Alicia's ladybug thing. Funny, the things you remember after someone is gone. Madison glanced toward the pool. She doubted Alicia ever got into the water that summer. It had probably always been too cold for her.

Madison walked past the pool and the park, then slowed down when she reached Alicia's street. The silver maples in front of Alicia's house were all grown tall now, and she could no longer see the wooden playhouse in the backyard. Pictures

kept appearing in Madison's mind, crowding her thoughts, making her realize the impact Alicia had had on her. Madison could see her second-grade self sitting on one of the tiny, white wooden stools in the playhouse, "eating" mud pies decorated with dandelions and clover from little plastic plates. She saw herself in Alicia's basement, where they had made up an imaginary wolf that could attack them anywhere except under the pool table, where they were safe. She saw herself marveling at her friend as she spoke fast, lyrical Spanish with her family. Madison's desire to be fluent in Spanish started in that house. Everything Alicia did had fascinated Madison. She had continually been amazed by Alicia's artwork, from the pop-up book about rabbits in second grade to the bold self-portrait in the style of Chuck Close in high school. Madison had first seen that painting displayed on an easel the Saturday after the crash. Numb with the news, she and Jessie, Julia, and Megan had gone to Alicia's house. Just that morning Madison had been at the DMV taking her driving road test. While Madison was waiting for her driver's license after passing the test, her mother called and told her what had happened. At first Madison thought it must have been another Alicia. It couldn't be her Alicia, the amazing artist, the genuine friend. But it was.

Madison still thought of her childhood friend almost every day. That's how she wanted things to remain. She wanted to be more like Alicia, a better artist, a truer friend. Recently

Madison had seen a quote that reminded her of Alicia, and she had shared it in one of the many letters she had been sending to Alicia's family over the past months. Eleanor Roosevelt once said, "Many people will walk in and out of your life, but only true friends will leave footprints in your heart." That was exactly what Alicia had done.

Madison felt fortunate to have these permanent footprints.

CHAPTER 13

Amanda

"Feliz, feliz en tu día,
 amiguita que Dios te bendiga,
 que reine la paz en tu día
 y que cumplas muchos más."

Amanda smiled, wiped the tears from her pale, delicate face, and put down her cell phone. She needed to concentrate on writing her college entrance essay, but she couldn't help herself. She had to listen to the saved birthday song again. Alicia's sweet-sixteenth birthday wish, something about having a blessed day filled with joy and peace. To hear her friend's voice, even when she couldn't understand the Spanish words, brought both joy and sadness. Amanda felt fortunate that she still had this reminder of Alicia and resentful that her friend had been taken away from her. Why Alicia? she still wondered. Why not him—the driver of the car—instead?

Amanda looked at her computer keyboard. She would never see her best friend again. Ever. She started to type. *I did not know when I awoke on September 25, 2004, that my life would forever change for the worse. . . .*

In the middle of the night Alicia's mother had called to ask if Amanda had the boy's phone number. His number was not in the school directory, and the operator said it was unlisted. Did Amanda know how to get in touch with him? Did she know any of his friends? Anyone who might have his phone number? If anybody knew these things, it had to be Amanda, Alicia's mom said. But Amanda didn't know Alicia was going out that night. She had seen the boy at the last football game, and she knew he and Alicia were becoming friends. That was all she knew.

I used to be constantly happy. . . .

From the moment Amanda met Alicia on the last day of Poms tryouts the summer before tenth grade, she loved her bright energy. They became friends, then best friends. Although they did not have any classes together, they hung out before school, during lunch, after school, and on weekends. Amanda loved their nightly, hour-long phone calls before dinner. They would talk about boys, school, and what they were going to wear the next day. Sometimes they even coordinated outfits. Alicia was so artistic in picking her outfits, and Amanda was always amazed that Alicia didn't care what people thought about how she dressed. Everything she wore looked good on her. Even red knee socks. Alicia said Amanda could wear anything she wanted as well, but Amanda didn't dare. What would others think?

On the Friday before Alicia turned sixteen, Amanda and Alicia met Vikki in downtown Rockville. It was a professional day at school, and classes were canceled. So the girls decided to go to the bargain matinee of *Mean Girls* to celebrate Alicia's birthday in advance. When the movie was over, they walked to the Tex-Mex restaurant next door to the theater.

"Let's sit outside," Amanda said as she lifted her red plastic tray from the counter. The afternoon was cool for the end of April, and the girls chose a table in the sun. Eager for summer to arrive, Amanda and Alicia were wearing flip-flops and Capri pants.

"Wait, wait! Let me take some pictures." Alicia pulled her camera from her tan purse. Amanda knew how much Alicia loved to take pictures. She had hundreds of photos stored in big, clear plastic boxes under her bed. To make albums with, Alicia had said. It was as if she needed to keep a record of every day of her life.

"What? Pictures of us eating?" Amanda said, laughing.

"Yeah. Make funny faces." Alicia looked through the viewfinder.

Amanda felt as if she were in a fast-food commercial, eating chips and salsa with faked glee alongside Vikki. *Click. Click.* They held their enchiladas in midair and paused for another picture. *Click.* Alicia put down her camera and made the monkey face that grossed out Amanda every time. Then Alicia crossed her eyes and rolled them back in opposite directions. Amanda joined in with her little tiger face. They ended up doubled over with laughter, gasping for breath.

When they calmed down they noticed a sleazy guy standing next to the movie theater entrance and staring at them.

"Let's get out of here," Vikki whispered. They slipped into Ben & Jerry's and bought two ice cream cones. They giggled and plotted what to do if the guy was still waiting outside when they left.

"We should go to the police," Vikki offered. "They have a station right around the corner."

"Oh my gosh!" Alicia licked her ice cream. "We should definitely go ask the police to protect us."

By the time they left the ice cream shop, the sleazy guy was gone. Good. Now it was Vikki's turn to shoot pictures. Amanda and Alicia stood back-to-back, chocolate and vanilla cones in hand, dipping their fingers into the dripping ice cream. *Click. Click. Click.* Another day recorded.

Another day etched in Amanda's mind.

———

After the accident I felt that I would never be happy again. A big part of me was missing. . . .

The Monday after the accident, Amanda froze in front of her locker. She felt herself sinking into a deep void. Someone came by and offered her another locker, at least for the first few weeks. Amanda thanked the person but said no. Then she forced herself to open her locker. The memories assaulted her.

"I can't open my locker," Alicia had complained. "I've been trying for ten minutes. I think it's broken." It was the first day of eleventh grade. Amanda and Alicia had been assigned lockers in the same hallway.

Amanda had heard the frustration in her friend's voice. "Come here. We can share," she said, moving her books to clear a shelf for Alicia. They already shared so many things that Alicia was almost like a sister to Amanda.

Spending time with Alicia was the main reason Amanda looked forward to going to school each day.

Then, over a weekend, that reason had vanished. But not Alicia's things. Not her schoolbooks, her Poms jacket, her hairbrush. They were all staring at Amanda from the top shelf of her locker. The locker became a constant reminder of how big the hole was in her heart, of how much she had lost. Sometimes Amanda got annoyed with all the kids in school crying, saying they missed Alicia. Some said they were best friends with her, but had they really known her? Had anyone been as close to Alicia as she?

It was difficult for Amanda to go on: There were so many reminders. A week after the crash, her math teacher reassigned seats. In the reshuffling, Amanda was seated right in front of the driver of the car. She felt a jolt in her chest when the teacher announced the change. Amanda didn't know what it would be

like when the boy came back to school and sat behind her. Actually she didn't even know if he would come back. Then three weeks later, there he was. He seemed just fine. Quiet, but fine. Amanda didn't befriend him. She couldn't, but she willed herself to be polite. In a way Amanda felt bad for him, knowing he would have to live with what had happened for the rest of his life. Still, why hadn't he been more careful? Why did he have to speed? Why couldn't he just have taken his time? His reckless driving had killed her best friend and left Amanda with—the void.

I felt this absence even more when I danced. . . .

The first Poms practice was unbearable. Alicia's place had been right beside Amanda in the dance routines. The coach said the spot would remain empty, as if Alicia were dancing there in spirit. Amanda swallowed hard. She looked at the empty space. It wasn't Alicia. It was just another void. Amanda was angry with herself for not believing in life after death. But she couldn't. No heaven or hell. No everlasting life. Thinking that there was nothing after you die was hard. It was so final.

When practice ended the squad sat in a circle. The girls talked about how they felt, getting stuff off their chests. Amanda said that for her, things would never be the same without Alicia. As Amanda talked, memories rushed back, and she broke down and cried. She hated crying, and how awful the whole session made her feel.

Amanda noticed that each time she talked about her friend, the void opened wider, ready to swallow her. So, eventually she stopped talking. She listened to others but kept her raw feelings to herself. Amanda became very good at concealing her emotions. Feelings hurt less if she kept them inside.

———————

Since her death my love of dance has only grown. When I dance, I do it for Alicia. . . .

Amanda began to dedicate every Poms performance to Alicia. Amanda did this in her head, for herself. At the beginning of eleventh grade, Alicia had written an essay nominating Amanda for captain of the squad. Alicia believed in Amanda, and that helped Amanda believe in herself. She wanted to dance her best, show her love of movement. She wanted people to feel joy from watching her perform, just like Alicia had made others happy when she danced. Amanda knew how much performing meant to Alicia. Dancing was a way of honoring her friend.

———————

She reread the last paragraph she had written. Amanda hoped this essay would help her get into the dance program at the college she had picked as her first choice. She knew she wanted to major in dance education. For the past five summers

Amanda had worked at a camp for special needs children. From the beginning she loved helping the kids, seeing them brighten and have fun when they danced. Sometime after Alicia's death, Amanda started to believe that each child she taught to dance would embody Alicia's spirit, her positive attitude toward life. Her students would be filled with light and joy when they danced, just as Alicia had been.

Funny, even though Amanda had thought she would never feel happy again, the closer she got to her goal, the happier she became. Little by little. Maybe some good could come from the bad.

She finished typing.

I think Alicia would be proud of me.

CHAPTER 14

Chad

Sitting on Alicia's bed, Chad opened last year's yearbook to the page he wanted. There she was. In a few weeks he would be graduating, and he couldn't stop thinking that Alicia would not be there. She had been there at preschool graduation. She had been there at elementary school graduation. She had been there at middle school graduation. All the way coming up, Chad had expected that Alicia would graduate from high school with him. She had always been there *with* him. She had always been there *for* him. He had often felt it was the two of them versus the rest of the class. He was black. She was Puerto Rican. They shared similar perspectives. He looked at the Social Studies spread in the yearbook, and his mind raced back in time. . . .

Advanced Placement Government was another class full of whites. Chad was watching the video on affirmative action along with everybody else. Alicia was a desk away. When the documentary got to the part where the Hispanic kids claimed that whites got better test scores because they were smarter, Chad had enough. He couldn't handle the lie. It touched a chord and made him angry. He got up and started to walk out of class. He had just reached the hallway when he sensed Alicia following him.

"Are you okay?" Alicia grabbed him by the arm, her warm touch instantly soothing him.

"What inspired Ms. Thomas to show that video?" Chad said, shaking his head. "You see our class. All white but us. The video's message is wrong." Chad looked into Alicia's eyes and saw his friend's support in them. "You agree, don't you?"

"You know I do."

Chad glanced back into the room. The video was finished, and class was going on as if nothing had happened. Chad had never shown any kind of disrespect to a teacher. This was the first time. He knew Alicia would not have walked out of a class. She was too polite. Yet here she was with him, not thinking about what the teacher or the other kids might say. She was always in his corner. The only time they argued was when Alicia told him about boys. Oh, man—boys.

———

Chad flipped through some pages of the yearbook in search of White Chad's picture. White Chad. Black Chad. Alicia had named them that way to distinguish them. . . .

"Why do you want to talk to him?" Chad was leaning against the hallway wall, his hands shoved deep in his pockets. "Why can't you talk to a Hispanic boy or a black boy?"

"He tells me he loves me and all these things."

"He's not good enough for you. He's not smart enough. He wears an earring! Alicia, you can't talk to this guy. He's trouble for you."

"What are you supposed to be, my big brother?"

"Yeah."

"But you haven't even met him."

Alicia had a point. Chad looked down. His shoelaces were untied, and he kneeled to tie them. He would spy. He would have to do one of his background checks to find out who this guy was friends with. Chad already knew he would always be skeptical, no matter how great this new boyfriend turned out to be. There was no one worthy of Alicia. She was brilliant, beautiful. She was a genuinely good person who wanted good for other people. No, no one was good enough.

––––––

A smile flickered across Chad's face. It turned out that there hadn't been much to worry about. White Chad had moved to Texas right before Christmas. Almost a year later he had come back, when he found out about Alicia's passing. Chad finally met him the day before the funeral. White Chad had shown up at school the Monday after the accident and pulled him out of class. Most of the school was in mourning, and the teachers had allowed kids to have some time to themselves. White Chad said Alicia had wanted them to meet. As the boys talked, Chad realized that White Chad was a nice guy after all. That afternoon the two of them had gone to the crash site, and they both ended up crying. . . .

Those first days after Alicia died, Chad cried uncontrollably. He had never cried before for anyone's death. Not his grandpa's on his father's side. Not his grandpa's on his mother's side. But now he didn't try to be tough, or say he was too old, or say he was a guy. He was distraught. He just had to let it out. Alicia meant that much to him.

During the funeral, when his eyes were so thick with tears he could hardly see, he heard a voice coming from the pew behind him. "Thank you for looking after her." The words gave him chills. God? Chad turned around and saw White Chad. It had been him. Or had it? Chad was moved by the thought that he had, indeed, been looking after Alicia since they were five years old. And God became real to Chad then because he knew someone he loved deeply was with him.

Chad started talking to Alicia whenever he prayed. He understood that Alicia could never be taken away from him. She was deep under his skin—the skin she used to draw on.

Chad looked at his hands resting on the yearbook and turned them palms up. . . .

On one of those school bus rides home in eighth grade, Alicia took Chad's arm and held it on her lap. Chad didn't pull away. He knew exactly what she was up to. She had done this so many times since they were little. She did it mostly in the classroom when they were sitting next to each other and the lesson got boring. She started to draw over the light skin on the palm of his hand. She drew lines that flowed and curled and opened into leaves and flowers that crept up his arm.

At home Chad took a shower, but the drawing remained.

"I see you've been sitting next to Alicia today," Chad's mother said, looking at his arm. "Can she make a drawing for me sometime?"

So the next day at school, Chad asked Alicia. She drew his mom a tiny, big-eared fairy on a piece of paper. It had long, wavy hair and large, pointy wings shaped like tulips. Chad's mom had been so pleased.

———

Chad turned the page of the yearbook. WHERE WILL YOU BE IN TEN YEARS? read the headline. . . .

Two years ago many of Chad's friends did not know what they wanted to do after high school. Not Alicia. She had a master plan. She wanted to go to art school to study interior architecture. She knew what she wanted to become. This was another reason why Chad loved her. She didn't have all the insecurities other girls had. Back in tenth grade Chad himself had a lot of questions about the future, about what to do when he graduated. After Alicia passed away, things changed. Chad thought about how easily he could have been the one who was dead. His and Alicia's lives had been similar in so many ways: They were minorities. They had older sisters who were the exact same age and much smarter than they were. Their parents were professionals and supportive of their kids. He and Alicia, they were two of a kind. But now there was only one of them. Chad had to live his life for both.

He started working harder and getting better grades in school. Then, early in his senior year Chad went to Atlanta to interview with one of the deans at Morehouse College. The dean asked Chad what he saw himself doing in ten years. Chad answered that he wanted to be a changer. He wanted to change things in the world that he felt were wrong, things that were not the way they should be. The dean told Chad he needed to keep in mind the difference between change and sustainable change. Chad had never thought about that. He realized then that Alicia had caused sustainable changes in people's lives. There were many people—kids and adults—who had known Alicia and could not go back to the lives they had been living before she passed away. That was the type of change that actually meant something. A lifetime in the larger scope of things was just a blip on the radar; but if you made a sustainable change, the change was alive. It lived on. That was important. Because they had known Alicia, Chad's class at Blake High School was wiser than most senior classes at other schools. His classmates questioned situations. Should I take this drink? Should I get in this car? Yeah, sustainable change.

———

Chad knew that he had changed in other ways too. When people talked about death, it was not a big, scary thing to him anymore. He still valued life. It would be disrespectful not to be thankful for what he had. Yet he was not afraid to die. Chad knew he had someone waiting for him.

He flipped some more pages. The Senior Class of 2005. There he was, the driver of the car. In the school picture, his eyes looked small behind his glasses. What had happened to that kid? Where was he now? Had he gone on to college? After the accident Chad checked out the guy. Chad found that he had tried out for the basketball team but didn't make it. He kept mostly to himself. Chad could not imagine how you go on, knowing you had caused someone's death. Had the kid's license been revoked? Thoughts like these would occur to Chad during his nights of insomnia. . . .

For so many months Chad tossed and turned, unable to sleep until his sister returned on the evenings she went out. He couldn't fall asleep until his girlfriend called to say she was home safe after being out late with her friends. Finally the day came when Chad was able to sleep again. He realized that everyone was put on Earth for specific reasons. He understood that there were a certain number of things people were meant to do for themselves and those they cared about. The fact that Alicia accomplished all she had in just sixteen years was very special. A lot of people live to be much older than Alicia and never deeply touch as many lives as she had, Chad thought. Even in death Alicia had brought the community closer. Old friendships were strengthened and new ones forged. Like his and Amanda's. They met shortly after Alicia died. It was meant to be, Chad figured, although on the surface he and Amanda couldn't be more different. He was a black Christian boy, and she was a white Jewish girl; but they clicked immediately. They were both captains of their teams, Varsity Basketball and Poms Squad. During the past two years they had become good friends. Chad saw Alicia in Amanda's smile. He felt Alicia's presence at school when the Poms danced.

———

And he felt Alicia's presence here, now, in this house, in her room.

"Dinner is ready!" Chad heard Alicia's mom call. He loved having dinner with Alicia's family. He had been to her house several times this past year. He closed the yearbook and bounded down the stairs. There would be no basketball team for him in college next year. Morehouse's full merit scholarship required that he maintain a 3.5 grade point average. Now that he had two names to bear—his immediate family's and Alicia's family's—he wouldn't have time to waste. He would focus on his studies. He would make both families proud.

Graduation crossed Chad's mind again. Lately, in a recurring dream, he was called to the stage to get his diploma. He couldn't see Alicia, but he felt her. He was certain she was there. Chad decided that he would take a photo of Alicia with him on graduation day. She would walk across the stage with him, in him.

Forever.

CHAPTER 15

The Driver

The Driver pushed his uncle's lawn mower up the hill, and his mind drifted again to *that night*. Almost two years now, and he still couldn't stop thinking about it. The haunting memories came back all the time, against his will. He would think, what if, on *that night*, he had stayed in. . . .

That night The Driver intended to stay home and catch up on his homework. Yeah. He was kind of behind in one class. This was the beginning of his last year of high school. He needed to do well because he planned to go to college. It was Friday, and The Driver thought he'd go to the new National Museum of the American Indian the next day, so he had to get his work done now. Then Brian called. There was this party out at Joey's house. Joey's brother, or someone, was celebrating his twenty-first birthday. It would be fun, Brian said. Brian was there already; and he pretty much forced him down, talked him into it. When The Driver arrived, he couldn't get in. Too many people were inside. So he called Alicia.

Alicia was the girl he liked since the very first time he'd noticed her at the HFStival the summer before his senior year. A pretty girl with a glistening smile. She was crowd-surfing in a bathing suit top and pants. That was the first time he had talked to her. Then when school started, he was so happy to see Alicia in his seventh-period Digital Arts class. He sat at the computer next to hers even though he was assigned to the Web design team and Alicia was on the theater advertising team. He couldn't resist. He had to be near her.

It had worked too. Alicia talked to him. She was like, "You're friends with one of my friends. Right?"

His heart skipped a beat. "Yeah, yeah. Justin."

That was the beginning of their friendship. Every day at the end of sixth period he waited at the bottom of the spiral stairway until he spotted Alicia. He would hurry over to carry her books and walk with her to Digital Arts. When class was over, he walked Alicia to her locker and then to Poms practice. On these walks they talked, her voice vibrant and bubbly, his hushed. They talked about everything that first week of school: college, careers, classes, whatever was on their minds. They just talked. He had known Alicia just one week, and she was telling him all these things. Wow! She wasn't doing it to impress him.

She was just being herself. No one outside his family had ever been this kind to him before, so nonjudgmental and willing to get to know him. Alicia hugged him!

One day they were talking about music, and he asked Alicia to come out to his car to listen to this CD he had just bought, the latest recording by Coheed and Cambria.

"Oh my gosh!" Alicia scampered across the parking lot. "Is this your new car?"

"Yeah." He opened the door of the Jetta and Alicia climbed in. "I'm paying for it. I put in three thousand of the eight thousand dollars my dad paid my cousin Vishal for it."

"Really? Where did you get the money?" Alicia asked.

The Driver rested his hand on the stick shift. "I've been working at this sign shop in Olney. It's the best-paying job I've ever had."

"How much do they pay you?"

"Nine dollars an hour."

"No way!" Alicia tapped her feet and nodded to the rhythm of the music. "You should get me a job there."

The Driver grinned. Life was good for him right now. He had a car. He was a senior bound for college. And he had a new friend—Alicia.

For three weeks straight, any chance he got, The Driver asked Alicia to hang out with him. That's why he called her when he wasn't able to get into the party *that night*. Once she had her parents' permission, he rushed over to pick her up.

On the way to her house he got lost. He called her again, and she gave him directions. Around eight forty-five he rang the doorbell and waited, smoothing his big T-shirt over his thin body. Alicia came out, glowing, clutching her small black purse under her left arm. Her mother appeared right behind her. The Driver had met Alicia's mother the night before, at Blake's home football game.

Alicia's mother leaned in the doorway and glanced at his car. "Are you a good driver?" she asked.

"I think so," The Driver replied. He adjusted his cap as he walked Alicia to the car. She looked so pretty. He couldn't believe he was finally going out with her. He was going to play *In Keeping Secrets of Silent Earth: 3*, the CD she had liked in the parking lot.

"Let's go to the Regal Cinemas in Rockville," he said once they were settled in the car.

"The Olney Theater is closer." Alicia signaled with her hand. "Oh, let me show you the best way to get out of my neighborhood." She went on to lead him to an entrance he didn't know. His uncle lived nearby, and he had always entered the Stonegate community by New Hampshire Avenue when he visited. "Every time you come to my house, come this way," Alicia added.

Every time. Even though she said they were only friends, maybe . . .

On the way to the movies, they picked up his friends Matt and Scott and dropped them off at Sole d'Italia. Outside the restaurant Charles, Brian, Justin, and George were waiting. The Driver liked that all his friends saw him with Alicia.

They arrived in time for the last show at the Olney. Toward the end of the movie The Driver asked Alicia if she had a curfew. She told him it was eleven thirty. He checked his watch. It was past eleven. He asked if she wanted to leave.

"No. Let's stay until the end. It's okay if I'm just a little late," Alicia said.

They came out of the theater to a still night. A three-quarter moon shone among the clouds. Alicia's silver bracelets jangled as she talked on the walk across the parking lot. After she got into the car, The Driver slid into his seat beside her. He grinned, wondering what would happen at her front door when they arrived at her house. The lot was nearly empty as he drove out of the Olney Shopping Center. Music blared from the CD player, filling the quiet evening. He glanced at Alicia. She looked so happy. Then he turned onto Spartan Road.

That was the last thing he remembered doing *that night*, even though his mind constantly tried to recover lost details. . . .

Three days later The Driver woke up in a hospital bed. His father was by his side. Tubes of all sizes were going in and out of his body. His mind was numb. It took a lot of effort to ask what had happened. His dad said he had been in an accident. He had crashed the car. For the past three days he had been in a coma. He had broken the T11 vertebrae in his spine and was lucky he wasn't paralyzed. He would have to wear a brace for a while. Did he remember anything, his father wanted to know. No, he didn't. Nothing. Absolutely nothing.

The Driver left the Shock Trauma Center and was transferred to a rehab facility. One afternoon he woke up feeling groggy. His father and a bunch of hospital people, including a psychiatrist, were standing by his bed. His dad spoke softly.

"Do you remember the girl in the car with you?" he asked.

"Yeah, Alicia." The Driver frowned, puzzled.

"She died in the crash."

"What!" The Driver's eyes popped open. "No! It's not true. I drove her home."

His dad started to explain how that wasn't the case.

"But I walked her to the front door," The Driver insisted. "She gave me a hug good-night. She did. I'm sure."

The psychiatrist interrupted to say that The Driver's mind was playing tricks on him. But The Driver remembered the warmth of Alicia's hug. He remembered her glistening smile. He remembered delivering her home safely and then driving away. How could he have imagined all that?

The time came when The Driver began to think of these memories as a dream. They couldn't be anything else. Overwhelmed by the facts, he started living in a fog. He couldn't focus on the simplest tasks. Things that had mattered before didn't matter anymore. Every time he thought about *that night*, he felt himself sink into a dark, bottomless hole, all alone. His stomach turned at the thought of going back to school. He heard the rumor that some of the boys were going to jump him when he returned. Still, he went back to Blake. He wanted to finish high school where he had started. But he didn't want to talk to anyone about what had happened. He was anxious about what people would think of him. He dreaded what they would say.

These fears were what kept The Driver from talking to Amanda in math for the rest of the fall semester. Even though he sat right behind her, he was never able to utter a word. What could he say, anyway? He knew she had been Alicia's friend. Alicia had introduced them at the last football game, where she had performed. He thought Amanda was mad at him. If he said something she might pour out all her hatred toward him. And she would be right to hate him. Alicia had died because of him. It had been his fault. So he kept silent, enveloped by the fog, his mind elsewhere, daydreaming.

The worst class was Digital Arts. He stared at the door the entire time, desperately wishing for Alicia to walk through it and end the nightmare.

School days became endless. He walked the crowded halls alone. He saw other kids staring at him and talking among themselves. At times someone would ask, "Are you okay?" But what was the person truly thinking? He didn't want people feeling sorry for him. He didn't like people knowing his name. He didn't want to be noticed at all. He wanted to be the kid he had been before *that night.* The quiet one in the back. He liked being that kid, but that kid was gone.

Shortly after the accident, Vishal drove him to the crash site. His cousin pulled over by the telephone pole, but The Driver couldn't get out of the car. He clenched his jaw, frozen in place. He couldn't make himself open the car door.

Later, he had no memory of what the crash site looked like then. Just a blank, like so many things that had happened after the accident. Impossible to remember.

Vishal suggested to The Driver that he keep a journal of his thoughts. For many months he did. He wrote so much and so often that he could not recall exactly when he started the letter of apology to Alicia's parents. Right after he had come out of rehab The Driver wanted to pay Alicia's parents a visit to tell them how sorry he was. He wanted to apologize. His dad and Vishal told him to wait, to get better first, to let things settle down. So he wrote his letter. It took him a long time to compose his thoughts and feelings into words. Mailing the letter gave him a small measure of relief.

I am responsible for the pain you felt when you first heard the news of your daughter's passing and I am responsible for the pain you feel now and the void in your lives. I go over in my head a hundred times a day, since I was first told the news of what had happened, how I could possibly tell you I am sorry. . . . I am not asking for your forgiveness. Just know that I am deeply and humbly sorry. . . . If you would like to talk, contact me.

The Driver went to the cemetery three times to pay his respects. Always with roses. On Alicia's eighteenth birthday he brought her orange ones. Brian drove him that day. When they arrived, the blue car was there. He knew it belonged to Alicia's father. The Driver waited until her father left. He could imagine the fury this man felt toward him. The Driver waited until the three girls who arrived right after Alicia's father also left. Only when he was sure no one else was coming did he get out of the car. He walked silently to the grave site and for the next half hour stood at the foot of the grave. He thought about what Alicia could have been. She had had so much ambition. He believed she was the better half of everyone she knew. She would talk to random people and then become friends with them. He had observed this. She had done this with him. She still amazed him.

The Driver continued to play the "what if" game over and over in his mind. He couldn't help it. What if Brian had not called *that night*? What if he and Alicia had gone to the movies in Rockville instead of in Olney? What if they had left the movie early? What if he had not taken the new way back to Alicia's house? If only one thing had been different, then he might not have crashed. At least, there was the possibility.

It took more than a year and a half before The Driver could bring himself to get out of the car at the crash site. He finally did it one night on his way home from a friend's house. It was almost eleven thirty; and, approaching the site, he felt like stopping. No one was around. He was curious. He wanted to see if he could jump-start his memory and recall what had actually happened. Why had he crashed? Had he really been speeding like the police said? Why hadn't he been wearing his seat belt when the rescuers came? He always wore his seat belt. He was sure he was wearing it *that night*, even though he didn't remember putting it on. His memories were still unclear about so many things, but not about the seat belt. The doctors said he must have been wearing it because he had been thrust forward and then pulled back by the force of the belt. That was how his spine had been fractured. Still, the police were convinced that he hadn't been wearing it.

The Driver got out of the car and crossed the road. Chills spread through his body and raised goose bumps on his skin. His breath became shallow. Here he was on the exact spot at the same time as the accident. The reminder of what had happened was devastating, a heavy weight he could not bear. He was creeped out. He hadn't known what to expect, what would happen next. There was a huge gap in his memory. He wanted the truth. He didn't want to make up things. The Driver was only able to stand a few minutes by the telephone pole before the urge to flee overtook him.

The lawn mower sputtered and stopped. He was done. Now the shouts of kids at the Stonegate pool became the background to his thoughts. Laughter. Happy kids. He wanted happiness too—a good job, a wife, two or three kids, the white picket fence, the American dream. He wanted to feel good about his life again, less sad, less guilty. . . .

Someone had suggested that talking with other teens about driver safety might help him. Those first few months at the community college he wanted to try that, but the thought also terrified him. He was afraid to tell his story, afraid of sinking again into that hole and not being able to get out. Each time The Driver talked about the accident, all those feelings welled up, and he got teary eyed. Why did it ever have to happen? he asked himself for the umpteenth time.

Karma. The Driver had grown up with the concept of karma, and he believed in it. He had been taught all his life that every action has a reaction: If you do good things you will be rewarded with more good things. If you do bad things, then they come back and bite you in the butt with more bad things. Yeah. It had been karma for him. He had sped. He had crashed. But Alicia hadn't deserved what she got. Not Alicia. She was good. He loved her so.

At first The Driver didn't know what to think about where Alicia had gone after she died. He just hoped she was in a better place than he was. Now he believed life ends when you die. He sure didn't want to know anytime soon where you go after death.

Sometimes he thought there were so many things he could have done to avoid the crash. It was all his fault, and this made him angry. Other times he wondered if a series of events had led to a higher event that was destined to happen, if that made any sense. This made him so sad. Still other times he felt the crash was just bad luck. Do dumb choices deserve this punishment? Karma. The fog again.

The Driver stored the lawn mower in his uncle's garage. Just last week The Driver had gone to the beach for a few days. He had been with friends. They had seen him smile. They thought he had been having fun. They hadn't known what he knew so well by now—the persistent, pervasive sadness, ready to rise to the surface every time he talked about

that night.

brought to the subject of your art. I have replayed on my head.
So your... life. In such a short I will always remember lady bug
time ___ ___ you created afternoons. I ___ am planting white
such amazing things. Your life daisies in your honor. ___
was to beautiful to be gone. I will gonna get something that will
always remember Drew. GT. last forever. A monument in
Dime's Rubberbands. ___ You, your honor. ___
Jessie V. Me: Dom. Everyday Just how beautiful you
another Chance to see you smile. were. how you'll live on
Everyday I will look for your soul. forever, In our hearts... In
Embrace the energy you let release our hearts. I love you &
into me. The impact you have on me I miss you...
is everlasting upon you. One of
these ___ brightest stars in the   You Were Stellar,
sky went out. I wrote the greatest
Drew I've ever written ___ all in   P.S. You always
your honor. Even after death,   will be. Here
you are inspiration as raw as   to 16 years of
the love. You   perfection. I
are indescribable.   can't say it enough.
You are...   I love & Miss you.
Wow. These
7 long years

Oh babe girl, little One...
6 years flashed, all the good times, your smile the most...
4wiz, French, everymorning, ET, the FA... what were you thinking...
the art... oh little one I love you
Alicia, took a while but I got it

✝
R.I.P.
Que
Dios te
Bendiga
R.A.P.

What can be said now that has not been said before?
What can be said now that will carry the weight of
our meaning, our feeling?
What can be said now, but that you were
joyful and joy-giving, that you
were loved and more worthy of it
than any

That you will be
sorely missed?

Let that, such, then,
be said.
You will be sorely missed.
Greek

Alicia, a few of us had a great girl
I had a few Saturday night.
the girls over on Saturday night. for class color
We made t-shirts Jess B. wrestling
day in your name, Jess B. wrestling
me about this movie about a bird. Coincidently
who is reincarnated as a bird. She's naming it
Jess found a bird in her house and
ended up keeping it. She's naming it
Alicia. On Friday during practice I'm
so glad you put me in a good mood.
I was having such a cruddy day +
you lightened me up. Ay, te quiero
tanto. Dejastes un ollo en mi
corazon. It's gonna be so hard
practice. I will miss you +
ya later.
        Te quiero mucho,
        ♡ Claudia

ALICIA -
I hope you
were aware of
how many people
truly + deeply
care for you. Life
will continue for
everyone, but for
people who never met
you, there will be some emptyness
because you filled all our lives
with love. ♡ m

Alicia,
I will never forget
you or your cartwheel

Love
George

Another
signature who
misses your
smile

CHAPTER 16

Mamá

Mamá pulled out a weed from among the pink impatiens bordering the stone patio, then glanced up at Alicia's bedroom window. Mamá remembered so many sunny afternoons just like this one. While she worked in the garden, Alicia would be in her room doing homework while listening to music through her headphones. When someone called and her daughter answered her cell phone, she would stand up, look out the window, and smile broadly at Mamá. Alicia would wave, her laugh cascading down in a bright tinkling of silver bells. To Mamá these moments were pure bliss, the love between them captured in one look, one gesture. These memories glittered in Mamá's mind, like Alicia herself. . . .

In the beginning Mamá had no idea how she would go

on living. She was an actress cast in the wrong movie, not knowing what to think and what to say, how to move and how to respond. "How do you host this party?" she asked a neighbor the Sunday after the crash when friends and family flooded her home with food and flowers.

For the first thirteen days Mamá felt as though she were living someone else's life, oppressed by the ever-present leaden cloud hovering above her. She went through the motions of life one day at a time, trudging along. In those brief moments when Mamá could look beyond herself, she saw her husband and older daughter in deep pain. She, who had always been there for them, felt utterly incapable of helping them. That she couldn't comfort those she loved so dearly tore at her.

Then one night Mamá had a dream, a dream so crisp and clear that she still remembered it in perfect detail almost two years later. In the dream Alicia, Verónica, Papá, and Mamá were running in a golden field among Yoshino cherry trees. The dark, sepia-colored tree limbs silhouetted against the cerulean blue sky were in full ethereal bloom *and* covered in autumn leaves. White petals and yellow leaves swirled gently to the ground. It was spring and fall at the same time, a beginning and an ending. The peculiar thing was that Mamá could see, talk to, and listen to her husband and older daughter; but she couldn't see or hear Alicia. She knew, however, that her younger daughter was playing with them. Alicia's presence was so strong.

The next morning when Mamá woke up, she felt like singing. She was singing later that morning when she went out to the garden to cut flowers for the first time since the crash two weeks earlier. A feeling of certainty possessed her. She knew Alicia was happy, that she lived on.

Mamá exhaled deeply as she arranged the mountain daisies in a vase. White daisies, she thought, like at the viewing.

Still in shock, Mamá had approached the casket with trepidation. A magnificent spray of fresh white daisies lay at its foot. The top was open for the family, as Verónica had requested. Alicia was dressed in the flowing ivory summer gown sprinkled with bunches of pink and lavender flowers that she had worn for her sister's nineteenth birthday party. On her long, thin neck was the freshwater pearl necklace she so loved to borrow from Verónica. Alicia's delicate hands had been placed one atop the other. Mamá looked at the slender girl so beautifully prepared for burial and understood immediately something she had only guessed before. This was not Alicia. It was just her body. Alicia's spirit was her true self, and her spirit could never die.

Mamá was sure that the previous night's dream had been Alicia saying, "I'm happy, Mami. You go on."

After the dream Mamá began to embrace anyone and anything that could remotely help her. She prayed with friends. She read all the books that came her way. She went to grief therapy and to a grief counselor. She put together the photo album of the preceding year, and cried at every picture that showed Alicia or their small family of four. She grieved deeply for what would never be but did not have one regret about what had been. She talked about Alicia with her daughter's friends and listened to every word they said. She found that talking about Alicia, sharing memories and learning things she had never known about her daughter, helped her heal. Mamá learned to be patient with herself, to allow grief to rise and be released whenever it had to be. Slowly she began to be grateful for the beauty in the world—a sunset, trees in bloom, a chipmunk burying fallen birdseed in a corner of her garden. And she began to laugh again.

Mamá witnessed changes in herself. She had gone through an event that shattered life as she had known it, and her priorities had shifted: She lost all fear of death and others' judgments. She was no longer afraid of being hurt, for there could not possibly be any pain deeper than that of losing a child. Her empathy grew. Mamá understood that everyone has hidden pain, and she sensed that each person had to follow his or her own path toward healing. She respected her husband's need to deal with his anger in his own way. She recognized Verónica's need to grieve in private over the loss of her only sibling, the one person who had shared her memories of growing up in their household. Her daughter's desolation made Mamá realize she also needed to strengthen ties with her own sisters. Through it all Mamá experienced sudden shifts in mood, zigzagging between a valley of tears and the peaks of joy. It was for the joyful moments that she chose to be totally present.

In time Mamá began to recognize the signs of a spiritual

connection to Alicia—a ladybug in the most unlikely of places, a previously overlooked message of love from Alicia written in one of Mamá's old day planners, the unexpected phone call from Chad on the first Mother's Day after the crash. And more vivid dreams. Mamá became acutely aware of all these surprising occurrences that seemed to carry messages. So she began to heed her inner voice: She learned to act on her instincts, following her heart instead of her head. When she went to Blake to pick up her daughter's artwork and crossed paths with The Driver that day—Alicia's seventeenth birthday—Mamá felt she was supposed to talk to him. Maybe he could tell her how Alicia had spent her last hours on Earth.

Then, more than a year after Alicia's death, Mamá received a letter from the dentist who lived on the hill overlooking the crash site. She knew there was a reason she needed to know him. *She would find out what it was.*

After reading the dentist's letter many times, Mamá picked up the phone one day and called him. She listened to Dr. Medina's story. That Friday night, he told Mamá, he was watching television in the family room of his house. From the room's large windows Dr. Medina had a clear view of the country road at the bottom of the hill. His backyard tapered onto the road's embankment. A little before eleven thirty he heard the sounds of a car out of control through the open kitchen window. He got up to look out and caught the movement of the car, heard the screeching of wheels, and saw headlights zooming into the embankment and back onto the road. Then he saw the car spin and heard it crash against the telephone pole. Trembling, he grabbed the phone off its stand on the kitchen counter. He ran out the side door of his garage and down the lawn toward the brush that marked the edge of his property. A young man who seemed to have some medical experience was relaying the kids' vital signs to someone on a phone. Inside the wreck, a boy was lying facedown across the backseat, his hands shaking. And strapped in up front in the brown Jetta, on the passenger side, was this beautiful young girl pinned by the bent metal, totally still. The dentist feared the worst, not knowing how to help but praying with all his heart that somehow she would come to life. Through her thick, long eyelashes he could see that her eyes were barely open, as if she were falling into a deep, deep sleep. Her brown hair was tied back in a ponytail, and bangs fell across her forehead. Around her neck was a silver chain with a heart pendant. When the dentist saw a tiny drop of blood trickling down the corner of the girl's mouth, he dabbed her face clean with the towel someone had handed him.

A week after the accident, Dr. Medina found out that the girl in the car—Alicia—was Puerto Rican, like himself. She was also the daughter of good friends of one of his dentist friends. By then Dr. Medina already knew that the driver of the car was from India, like his wife, who happened to know of the boy's family. Dr. Medina didn't know what to make of these connections. He was puzzled by the coincidences, and tormented by the fact that he was not able to do anything for Alicia on that awful Friday night.

For many months after the accident, Dr. Medina said, he was haunted by Alicia's image. He kept wondering how it was possible that her expression showed no signs of pain or struggle, almost as if she had never been present at the wreck. He was plagued by flashbacks and nightmares, from which he would wake up sobbing silently. Not finding solace for almost a year, Dr. Medina considered selling his house to flee the scene of the crash at the foot of his backyard. Finally he felt compelled to get in touch with Alicia's parents. *I can still see her angelic face in my mind and get teary eyed every time I think of her and recall what happened*, he had written.

Mamá pondered Dr. Medina's story long and hard. Initially she couldn't understand why he had brought the crash back into her family's life at a time when some normalcy had been reestablished. She saw the deep pain resurface in her husband, and this made her very sad. She knew, however, that she would understand in time; and soon that understanding came. The one thing that still tugged at Mamá's heart was that Alicia had been alone at the moment of her last breath. How Mamá had wished for one final kiss, one more *te quiero mucho angelita* to send her daughter off with the complete knowledge of being cherished. The truth was that a total stranger had given Alicia what no one in her family could at that moment. Dr. Medina had given to Mamá's little angel what Alicia had shared with all who crossed her path—genuine love. Mamá believed he had loved Alicia with the pure, unconditional love of one human being for another at the precise moment her spirit left her body.

Mamá felt such comfort from this realization. She wrote back to Dr. Medina to describe her insight. Much later, he told her that what she described in her letter had made the flashbacks and nightmares stop.

Two mourning doves splashed in the waterfall, and a tiny frog sunbathed on a lily pad. Mamá sat on the weathered teak bench by the pond under the Japanese maple tree and took off her straw hat. A squirrel climbing up the papery bark of a river birch made her look up, and she breathed in the sweet scent of daylilies. These days—two months shy of the second anniversary of Alicia's death—Mamá felt mostly proud and grateful. She was proud of being Alicia's mother. She believed Alicia had accomplished what she was supposed to in life. She hoped that as a result of Alicia's accident, many teenagers were now more careful on the road and that the adults in their lives were more aware of the dangers of teen driving. Mamá knew she was blessed with the love of family, friends, and total strangers who had helped her heal in a myriad of ways. She was grateful for Alicia's friends, who had so loved her daughter and in whom she now saw bits and pieces of her. Mamá was comforted by the certainty that there were still four members in her immediate family. The bond of love had never broken, so how could Alicia cease to be?

And The Driver? Mamá had hugged him. He had woken from his coma convinced that he had walked Alicia to her front door and delivered her home safely. He *remembered* her warm hug. Mamá believed that Alicia had visited The Driver in a dream. If Alicia could do that—release him—why shouldn't Mamá? He was so young and inexperienced.

A light breeze blew through the garden, and the song of the wind chimes brought back last Sunday morning. . . .

Mamá closed her eyes during the meditation exercise, and to her total astonishment she saw Alicia as if she were alive. Mamá was certain this was not just a memory, or something imagined, or even the silhouette of Alicia she had seen so many times before. This was her younger daughter's smiling face in the flesh, in full color and three dimensions. Mamá could almost touch her.

The image stayed for only a few seconds, lit against the dark of her eyelids. When it vanished, Mamá shed tears of joy.

She felt light, warm, and very loved.

¡Alicia! Gracias angelita.

AUTHOR'S NOTE

On the evening of September 24, 2004, my younger daughter, Alicia María Betancourt, was killed in a car crash. Alicia was one of seventeen teenagers who died in car accidents in the Washington, D.C., suburbs that fall.

Alicia was a sixteen-year-old junior at James Hubert Blake High School in Silver Spring, Maryland. After the funeral mass I stood next to my husband and older daughter, Verónica, by the door of the church, hugging and greeting what seemed to be a never-ending line of people. Like my husband, I was struck by the hundreds of teens who were so touched by Alicia's passing and the fact that these teens were from a broad spectrum of racial, ethnic, socioeconomic, and religious backgrounds. In the ensuing months of shock, pain, and grief, some questions kept demanding answers. Who was Alicia to her friends? How were they dealing with the loss? Why did this happen?

Sometime in November 2004 I finally gathered the courage to start calling some of Alicia's friends to talk about her. I had a vague idea of wanting to write some sort of memoir of Alicia as seen through her friends' eyes. I bought a small tape recorder and, with permission, recorded the conversations I had with these young people.

The interviews with twenty-two of Alicia's friends were held mostly in my sunlit studio and took place over the next year and a half. I spoke with many of the teens more than once. I asked the expected questions, such as: What kind of friend was Alicia for you? How did you find out about the crash? And I asked more unusual questions: Have you ever felt her presence after she died? Do you think there was a reason for her death?

As the interviews progressed, I learned how isolated teens feel in their grief. I discovered how individualized their reactions are to the death of a loved one and that teens have very few models for dealing with their pain. I also learned that healing takes patience and time. Eventually I realized that the stories I had heard from Alicia's friends might bring some comfort to others.

The final selection for the book came down to thirteen young voices. I wanted to keep most of the chapters and the book as a whole short, to mirror the time Alicia had spent on Earth. From experience I also know that when a person is grieving, it is hard to concentrate on anything for a long time. I thought that limiting the length of the chapters would make the book more accessible to those who are dealing with the pain of losing someone they love.

Before I started to write each of Alicia's friends' chapters I listened to that person's interviews over and over in an effort to capture his or her voice and the nuances of the feelings expressed. Although all the chapters in the book are based on my interviews, I fictionalized some material. At times I had to place these young people in situations and settings that led them to have their many memories of Alicia. For that to happen I either created some of the dialogue that gave way to a particular recollection or I imagined the interior monologue that triggered the memory. In some cases I combined the memories of several young people to give richness and depth to specific recollections.

Even though I took some liberties to round out individual chapters, the feelings and events portrayed are as accurate as I can recount them. I treated the stories told to me with great respect, and I am incredibly grateful to all Alicia's friends for their time, candor, and willingness to share their most personal thoughts, feelings, and emotions. Most especially, I feel blessed by the love they bestowed on Alicia.

I am writing this note almost four years after that terrible Friday. I believe that if this book helps bring some solace to others who must endure grief or if it illuminates for young readers the consequences of speeding and driving without enough experience, it will have achieved its goal.

That will be Alicia's legacy.

ABOUT THE TITLE

For the first six months after the crash, every time I closed my eyes I saw a luminous silhouette of Alicia's smiling face against the dark of my eyelids. During that time I was calling the manuscript for this book *Alicia: Brushstrokes*. One afternoon I was riding in a taxi with my husband and Verónica, discussing the manuscript. Verónica told me that the title needed to be changed, that it was trite and teens would not respond to it. I leaned against the backseat of the taxi and closed my eyes, seeing once again Alicia's silhouette. I opened my eyes and asked my husband, an ophthalmologist, what the English word was for the phenomenon I was experiencing. His answer was immediate. I was seeing an afterimage. As soon as I decided to change the title of the book to *Alicia Afterimage*, I stopped seeing Alicia's face. It was as though Alicia had been telling me the title of the book all along.

ALMOST FOUR YEARS LATER...

Erin is a sophomore at the University of the Incarnate Word in Texas. She is a member of the synchronized swimming team and plans to major in chemistry in the pharmacy school. Erin still wears the heart pendant, and always has the frame Alicia made in her room.

Corrina is a sophomore at Tufts University in Massachusetts, majoring in art history and psychology. She thinks about Alicia often and continues to be inspired by Alicia's creativity, talent, and passion for life.

Gaeb is a junior at Montgomery College in Maryland, where he leads the Urban Dance & Lifestyle group. He still has Alicia's birthday card pinned to the wall in his bedroom.

Kathlynn is a sophomore at Towson University in Maryland. Her car keys hang from a ladybug key chain. To this day nobody is allowed to touch her knee.

Colin is a sophomore at Loyola Marymount University in California. A film major, he would like to become a director of photography, overseeing the camera and lighting crews working on movies.

Lauren is a sophomore at the University of Wyoming. She is an English major and plans to go to law school after graduation. She has had the recurrent dream of Alicia at least eight times.

Nikki is a sophomore at The Peabody Institute of the Johns Hopkins University in Maryland, where she is a classical percussion major. She would like to pursue a career in music therapy, developing new treatments or simply performing for and teaching those who find relief in music.

Ben is at the University of Maryland. He plays the acoustic guitar on a regular basis and fiddles with the songs he has composed through the years. The only work he thinks is just right is "A Perfect Mourn," the song he wrote for Alicia.

Vicky is a sophomore at Northeastern University in Massachusetts. She is majoring in journalism with a minor in human services. She loves volunteering in the service of others, mentoring foreign students, and tutoring inner-city kids. Twizzlers are still a favorite candy.

Madison is a Latin American studies major at Boston University. She speaks Spanish fluently and sees herself working for a nonprofit organization involved in Latin America after she graduates.

Amanda is a sophomore at East Carolina University in North Carolina, majoring in dance education. She keeps a portrait of Alicia by her bedside, and not a day goes by in which she doesn't think of her friend.

Chad is at Morehouse College in Georgia. He is an English major minoring in economics and plans to go on to law school. Chad still talks to Alicia in his prayers. He tries to remember her in everything he does and often thinks about the days when Alicia used to draw on his skin.

The Driver is at Montgomery College in Maryland, studying economics. He has started to tell his story publicly in the hope that others won't make the same mistakes he made.

SELECTED RESOURCES
ON TEEN GRIEF

Organizations and Web Sites

THE DOUGY CENTER FOR GRIEVING CHILDREN AND FAMILIES provides a place for grieving children, teens, young adults, and families to share their stories. The center serves as a model and educational training center for support groups around the United States.
Web site: dougy.org

JOURNEY OF HOPE GRIEF SUPPORT CENTER offers support for children, teens, young adults, and their families as they deal with grief and mourn the death of a loved one.
Web site: johgriefsupport.org

MOMMY'S LIGHT LIVES ON provides services to families in which the mother is dying or has died, with an extensive Bereavement Education and Outreach Program offering information and educational materials for grieving children and teens.
Web site: mommyslight.org

Books

Fitzgerald, Helen. *The Grieving Teen: A Guide for Teenagers and Their Friends*. New York: Fireside, 2000.

Gootman, Marilyn E., Ed.D. *When a Friend Dies: A Book for Teens About Grieving & Healing*. Minneapolis: Free Spirit Publishing, 2005.

Helping Teens Cope with Death. Portland, OR: The Dougy Center, 1999.

SELECTED RESOURCES
ON TEEN DRIVER SAFETY

Organizations and Web Sites

AMERICAN ACADEMY OF PEDIATRICS provides guidelines for a Parent-Teen Driving Agreement setting forth specific rules that teen drivers must follow.
Web site: aap.org/publiced/BR_TeenDriver.htm

INSURANCE INSTITUTE FOR HIGHWAY SAFETY is dedicated to reducing property damage, injuries, and deaths from vehicle crashes on United States highways.
Web site: highwaysafety.org *or* iihs.org

NATIONAL SAFETY COUNCIL'S Teen Driving division works to develop driver experience and skills, reduce teen drivers' exposure to risk, and modify risky driving behavior for the prevention of accidental injury and death.
Web site: nsc.org/issues/teendriving

Books

Berardelli, Phil. *Safe Young Drivers: A Guide for Parents and Teens.* Vienna, VA: Nautilus Communications, 2006.

Loughry, John H. *Saving Our Teen Drivers: Using Aviation Safety Skills on the Roadways.* Ashland, OH: Seminee Publishing Ltd., 2005.

Smith, Timothy C. *Crashproof Your Kids: Make Your Teen a Safer, Smarter Driver.* New York: Fireside, 2006.

Teen Driver: A Family Guide to Teen Driver Safety. Itasca, IL: National Safety Council, n.d.

ACKNOWLEDGEMENTS

Many people helped make this book a reality.

Erin, Corrina, Gaeb, Kathlynn, Colin, Lauren, Vikki, Ben, Vicky, Madison, Amanda, Chad, Kevin, Cameron, Natalie, Jessie, Julia, Rachel, Renee, Kathryn, and Jessica—thank you for opening your hearts and minds. I see bits and pieces of Alicia in each one of you.

Thank you also to The Driver, who answered all my questions to the best of his ability. May your healing continue.

To Dr. Medina, who opened his home and heart to me in an effort to help. Thank you.

I am very grateful to Jennifer Barrett O'Connell, Janet Morgan Stoeke, and Susan Stockdale, the members of my critique group. These authors and illustrators of books for young people are also the friends who read, critiqued, wept, and endured with me while I struggled to give shape to the novel.

To Louise May, my editor, thank you for the sensitive way in which you helped me revise and polish such a personal story. To Lee & Low Books, my gratitude for undertaking yet another risk.

Thank you to Maria Salvadore, Children's Literature Specialist, who, from the very beginning, encouraged me to proceed and pointed out the possibility of making the book accessible to both young adults and adults. And thanks to Judith Ortiz Coffer and Rosemary Brosnan for their support and advice in the quest for a publisher.

Dr. Mimi Mahon, Advanced Practice Nurse in Palliative Care and Ethics, who was the generous soul who reviewed the sources cited in the manuscript, thank you.

Heartfelt thanks to my friend Pat Swanson, with whom I worked through my feelings about the interviews during our long walks.

To my daughter Verónica, my first reader, whose advice was instrumental in learning to write for teens. And to Arturo, my husband and friend for almost three decades, thank you for your support and enduring love. Thank you both for understanding how important it is to me that our story helps others. I am blessed that you are part of my life.

Believe